Trust: A Shock to the System
A Practical Guide

TRUST: A SHOCK TO THE SYSTEM
A PRACTICAL GUIDE

RICHARD DEAN SMITH

Kroshka Books
New York

Senior Editors: Susan Boriotti and Donna Dennis
Coordinating Editor: Tatiana Shohov
Office Manager: Annette Hellinger
Graphics: Wanda Serrano
Editorial Production: Maya Columbus, Vladimir Klestov,
Matthew Kozlowski and Tom Moceri
Circulation: Ave Maria Gonzalez, Vera Popovic, Luis Aviles, Raymond Davis,
Melissa Diaz, Magdalena Nunez, Marlene Nunez and Jeannie Pappas
Communications and Acquisitions: Serge P. Shohov
Marketing: Cathy DeGregory

Library of Congress Cataloging-in-Publication Data
Available Upon Request

ISBN: 1-59033-646-1.

Copyright © 2003 by Kroshka Books, An Imprint of
Nova Science Publishers, Inc.
400 Oser Ave, Suite 1600
Hauppauge, New York 11788-3619
Tele. 631-231-7269   Fax 631-231-8175
e-mail: Novascience@earthlink.net
Web Site: http://www.novapublishers.com

All rights reserved. No part of this book may be reproduced, stored in a retrieval system or transmitted in any form or by any means: electronic, electrostatic, magnetic, tape, mechanical photocopying, recording or otherwise without permission from the publishers.

The authors and publisher have taken care in preparation of this book, but make no expressed or implied warranty of any kind and assume no responsibility for any errors or omissions. No liability is assumed for incidental or consequential damages in connection with or arising out of information contained in this book.

This publication is designed to provide accurate and authoritative information with regard to the subject matter covered herein. It is sold with the clear understanding that the publisher is not engaged in rendering legal or any other professional services. If legal or any other expert assistance is required, the services of a competent person should be sought. FROM A DECLARATION OF PARTICIPANTS JOINTLY ADOPTED BY A COMMITTEE OF THE AMERICAN BAR ASSOCIATION AND A COMMITTEE OF PUBLISHERS.

Printed in the United States of America

To
Maudelle Terry

CONTENTS

Acknowledgments		xi
Preface		xiii
Chapter 1	**Shock to the System**	1
	A. Introduction	1
	B. A Shock to the System	3
	C. The Two Most Difficult	4
	D. The Socio-Economically Advantaged or *The Sick-Sybarite Syndrome*	6
	E. The Disadvantaged, Medicaid	12
	F. Mom's List	15
	G. Sign of the Yellow Tablet	16
Chapter 2	**Complaints**	19
	A. The Complainer	19
	B. The Complaint	21
	C. The Angry, Upset Complainer	24
	D. The Help-Rejecting Complainer	26
	E. The Habitual Complainer	29
	F. The 'Why' Question	31
Chapter 3	**Confrontation**	35
	A. Street Fight	35
	B. Intimidation	37
	C. The Hateful Patient	39
	D. Virulent Visitors. The Schmoo Enigma	41
	E. Managed Care Monster	44
	F. The Telephone Terrorist	45
	G. Bad News	47

Chapter 4	**Big Shot**	**49**
	A. Return of the Sybarite:	
	The Neglected Parent Constellation	49
	B. Big Shot from Out of Town	51
	C. The Famous Person Constant	53
	D. The Machiavelli Principle: or	
	The Toxic Healthcare Professional	54
Chapter 5	**Passive Distrust**	**57**
	A. The Guilt / Shame Duality	57
	B. "Thanks Anyway, Doc."	60
	C. Splitters and Squatters	64
	D. The Alternative Medicine Parry	66
	E. The Absolutist	69
Chapter 6	**Futility**	**71**
	A. Informed Consent: "You're the Doctor."	
	Bounded Rationality	71
	B. Personality Conflict	74
	C. The Dooney-Bourke Boundry	75
	D. Disgust Leads to Distrust	76
	E. Pillar to Post: From the Borderline and Beyond	78
Chapter 7	**Rehab Milieu**	**81**
	A. Emily's Hair	81
	B. Cats and Dogs: Homesickness	83
	C. 'Crisis' at 7 to 10 Days: Italian Prozac	86
	D. Family in Crisis	88
	E. "She's a Fighter"	89
	F. The Vanishing Family	91
Chapter 8	**Physicians and Conflict**	**93**
	A. Physicians and Conflict	93
	B. Fear	95
	C. "My Former Doctor"	98
	D. "If You Want to Be My Doctor!"	99
	E. Flattery	100
	F. "And How Are *You*, Doctor?"	102
Chapter 9	**Conclusions**	**105**
	A. The Socially Inept	105
	B. Ray Charles: "The Snake"	108

C. A Word for It: Rebarbative	109
D. Additional Guidelines	111
E. Conclusion	113
Index	**117**

Acknowledgments

My appreciation to members of the Rehabilitation Team at John Muir Medical Center, Walnut Creek, California who together we experienced the exasperations that led to development of ideas that made practicing medicine possible under sometimes difficult circumstances. All followed on the invaluable advice of Maudelle Terry who gave us hope that we could survive and work with these distrustful individuals. My gratitude to Sandra Percario who read and greatly improved the manuscript. And thanks to Librarian Helen Doughty for gathering obscure materials, her support, and valuable suggestions.

PREFACE

Gaining a patient's trust, or the trust of a patient's family, may seem to be a given, but achieving trust is a fragile, individual, hazardous endeavor. In an era of distrust of institutions and professions, the patient must trust the staff of doctors, nurses, and therapists before a working therapeutic relationship can be established.

In recent decades, coping with angry and difficult people produced numerous books, consultants, and seminars. *Trust: A Shock to the System* approaches the issue from the standpoint of developing a working, trusting relationship with patients and families, and the pitfalls that one may encounter. We discover that the individuals–patients, family members, visitors–behave in circumstance of illness in the same manner they behave in other aspects of their lives: at home, at the grocery store, at the airport, etc. While most people are reasonable, given their trying circumstances, a small number are distrustful, difficult, and consume inordinate time and energy of the staff.

The angry and distrustful individuals try to make our staff and therapists responsible for how they feel and what has happened to them. Chaos is their element, and creating chaos their specialty. From the "Angry Big Shot from Out of Town" to "Toxic HealthCare Professional from Away" to "The Sick Sybarite Syndrome" and "Virulent Visitors," patterns of behavior evolve, making understanding and management possible with better outcomes and less stress on the staff. Everyone must help in management because splitting the staff, turning one staff member against the other, threatens our ability to care for patients and to maintain staff morale.

Most interactions with troublesome people in a medical setting are brief, but on a Rehabilitation Unit we live with and must deal with these situations for longer periods, often weeks. For the functioning of our Unit, controlling and managing these incendiary situations becomes imperative. Cost constraints by private and public agencies make it more pressing, especially in protecting our staff and maintaining our mission to provide appropriate medical services.

Theorists call it 'reciprocal altruism,' that is, people tend to be pleasant to people who are pleasant to us, and disagreeable with those who are disagreeable to us. Reciprocal altruism may be fine in a medical setting, reciprocal disagreeableness is not, although one's instincts urge otherwise.

Taking control of these problematic situations may determine the success of patient management and success of a Unit of the hospital. If a troublesome situation is handled well, a distrustful, complaining individual often becomes our greatest ally. No one is all bad all of the time. Some individuals are complaining and distrustful as a matter of behavior style, or habit, and are not especially virulent; others intent on inflicting harm.

Trust: A Shock to the System outlines situations and problem individuals that we encounter and how to cope with them. *Trust* is not an academic study, but a practical guide. The recommendations presented developed from trial and implementation in daily practice. *Trust* concentrates on behavior and its management in a medical setting with no attempt at analysis.

Trust: A Shock to the System is Street Wisdom come to the bedside.

Chapter 1

SHOCK TO THE SYSTEM

A. INTRODUCTION

"Man is not [first and foremost] a reasoning animal; he is a feeling, contemplating, acting animal."

John Henry Newman.[1]

Most encounters of doctors and other medical providers with patients and families are relatively brief. In the office, contact may be less than 15 minutes and at the hospital a duration of stay only a few days. Problems of communication and development of trust and rapport between patients and their families with the medical staff are sometimes difficult, but end with the patient being discharged with or without resolution of behavioral problems. Follow-up visits in the doctors' offices also tend to be brief. In some instances, the only way that seems feasible to deal with these problematic, distrustful individuals is to terminate contact promptly. And if they are referred from out of town, to send them back home as soon as possible.

On an Acute Rehabilitation Unit, a patient's length of stay is longer, averaging two to three weeks. The difficulties in managing patients and their families must be dealt with on the spot and don't go away in a short time, nor can they be discharged at an early date or any other way to circumvent difficult situations.

---

[1] David G. Schultenover. "George Tyrrell: Devout Disciple of Newman." M.E. Allsopp and R.R. Burke, editors. *John Henry Newman: Theology and Reform*. New York and London: Garland, 1992, p. 72.

Experience dealing with a host of difficult to impossible situations may help others in their encounters with these difficult and distrusting patients. Individuals covered in this case make up only a small per cent of patients and family members, probably less than 5 per cent, but take up 90 per cent of energy in coping with day-to-day conflicts that arise from their behavior.

A few references are cited, but nearly all examples come from office experiences or wards of the hospital and the Acute Rehabilitation Unit. No scientific claims are made and this discussion will not satisfy evidence-based practice, or any other attempt to codify vagaries of human nature. Nor do I claim a systematic clinical data collection, but include situations that keep doctors and nurses and therapists awake at night, that aggravate waking hours, and cause one to wonder why anyone would choose such a career, that is, empirical, based upon experience and observation alone without science or theory. Yet, to survive a truly ornery, cussed, outrageous patient or relative requires resourcefulness, patience and imagination. Street wisdom learned the hard way is what I present, and without a guide or mentor to soften the bewilderment and sense of failure and frustration that accompanies these individuals.

Nor do I claim that these are the only examples of chaotic behavior that we are exposed to and must make the best of. New varieties are likely to arise with the changing scene, which in my estimation, does not change very much. Both patients and family members are considered, as well as visitors who may assume excessive claims to the staff's time, energy and patience.

Most people are reasonable and able to trust most of the time, but those individuals who are outliers, three or four standard deviations off the norm of human behavior, under the stress of illness, require an extraordinary amount of time and energy from an already stressed staff. We must cope with the distrustful, but we seldom talk about these difficult, distrustful and sometimes threatening individuals amongst ourselves; rather we suffer and endure them unnecessarily by ourselves. The problem is timeless as recorded in the world's literature. Broad categories and a general outline are presented, acknowledging that many exceptions arise. Some exhibit multiple aspects of distrust.

People and characterizations discussed cross all lines of race, color, creed, religion, code, gender, pledge of allegiance, or country of origin. While dealing with difficult people has become a major enterprise, the undermining of trust is the outcome and end result of many of these trying encounters.

It's the Law of the Jungle brought to the bedside. Out of the wreckage of human behavior comes valued experience leading to maneuvers and tactics of survival that are appropriate to almost all aspects and settings of human interaction: schools, families, teams, corporations, etc. To those who find my descriptions and experience meliorative to their daily coping with the difficult and distrustful, I say hurrah! For those who don't, I say good luck, anyway.

B. A Shock to the System

In my early days of practice, I was called to attend the elderly patriarch of a multi-generational immigrant family. He was bedfast in Intensive Care Unit with a complex medical and surgical illness. In meeting with the family, I was surrounded by semicircles of the gentleman's immediate and extended family. Each row towards the outermost semicircle represented a younger generation like the rings of the trunk of sapling tree, it seemed five or six deep. At the outside row stood mothers who rocked babes in arms. Each row edged closer to hear my words. The spokesman was a young man who was the only one present more or less fluent in English.

I patiently explained the anatomy, physiology, biochemistry, and therapeutic interventions both medical and surgical as plainly as I possibly could. A full explanation in the highest discharging of my duty, supported by modern law and millennia of ethics of my profession, I fulfilled my obligation *in toto*.

My efforts were greeted with doubt and distrust, a restiveness, and impatience that began to unnerve me. I retraced my explanations, making small revisions wherever I thought clarity might have faded. The rows of generations seemed to close in, frowning faces searching for meaning in my, to them, largely incomprehensible explanations, verbal diagrams, measured gesticulations, and efforts at reassurance.

The hallway grew warm, humidity uncomfortable, beads of moisture collected on my brow and lip, my mouth became dry, my voice grew tense and husky, and my knees began to misbehave by seeming not willing to support my narration either. I began to stammer. I looked at each member of each row, pleading to see someone who could relate to me that they understood and appreciated my heroic efforts in their behalf. A nod. A smile. A sigh. The babes-in-arms cried ever more stridently wriggled against their mothers' comforting arms.

At last, from some unknown depth, nook, cranny, or crevice of my lost consciousness or unconsciousness, I blurted, "It was a shock to his system."

I have no idea what a shock to the system might entail, but I had heard it sometime in the past not knowing that I might one day be called upon to speak it. I couldn't possibly give an explanation of such a system-shock.

The young man, the spokesman, held his breath a moment, then sighed. A look of relief drifted across his face. He faintly smiled, and turned to the assembled multitude of generations. The young man nodded, and smiled to the others, repeating in several tongues, "It was a shock to his system." A wave of relief and satisfaction rippled gently from the front generations towards the most rearward members. The babes-in-arm were silent for an ever so brief instant, then resumed in a most agreeable and pacific lamentation.

The multitude drew back somewhat, shuffled their feet in relief. The way parted, and I passed through the rift, like I was entering Parliament. Members of the family made courteous gestures that I was, 'all right.'

From that point on, whenever I entered the gentleman's room in ICU, children were abruptly scat out into the hallway and hushed. When I approached the gentleman's bed, all living and inanimate objects were summarily, brusquely pushed aside. When I reached for something, a glass, a cup, a corner of the sheet, a hand would quickly reach it for me. I was thanked profusely. I examined his tongue, eyes, chest, heart and all the rest. I completed my visit, and with some ceremony, departed to be greeted in the same manner again at each visit.

"A shock to the system."

I have no comprehension what it means. Certainly, I did not communicate any meaningful knowledge. I could not give an explanation of the anatomy, physiology, or other educational information of such a shock. Nevertheless, I accomplished something that was as important and perhaps more important than full disclosure: I gained their trust. Not by pontification, or lecturing, or rudeness, or bluffing, but by–I'm not sure what.

Some tetchy ethicists might cry "paternalism!" True enough, but I tried their restrictive ways and failed. I tried a different way and succeeded, succeeded in gaining their trust. Which is more important? I say gaining trust, for without trust, we can do little. With a trust, we can work together.

C. THE TWO MOST DIFFICULT

The two categories of distrustful people we most commonly see on the Rehabilitation Unit are those who are socio-economically advantaged and those who are socio-economically disadvantaged. They are surprisingly alike. Both live and exist in competitive hierarchical social systems. Both systems are built on inefficiency and distrust. Both require a large measure of ingenuity in working-the-system, or "the squeaky wheel gets the grease," and other similar admonitions of survival in an often hostile, impersonal, dog-eat-dog world.

At the same time, we are witnessing the disappearance of the middle income families. We wonder 'where did all of the reasonable people go?' The middle income or middle class people tend to be less difficult and more trusting than either the advantaged or disadvantaged. [Marketers refer to the middle income or middle class as 'middle brand.'] Members of the middle class work hard, pay their bills, hold jobs for long periods, and are honest, law-abiding, reliable, salt-of-the-earth citizens. They work well with the medical and therapy staff, respect working together toward a common goal of gaining independence, and are respectful towards professionals. In addition, middle income individuals tend to keep appointments, communicate in a forthright manner, accept advice, and follow through with instructions on care, and express appreciation.

Over the last half of the twentieth century, the lower income working class increased from thirty to forty per cent of the population. The affluent increased from ten per cent to thirty per cent of the population. At the same time, those in the middle income group fell from sixty per cent to thirty per cent of the population; called a shift towards a 'bi-modal society' of high and low income population: the two classes that are the most difficult grew from forty per cent of the population in 1950 to seventy per cent by 2000, with a marked reduction in the number of people with middle incomes.

Medicine, largely undifferentiated in its focus, tends towards the middle class or middle brand. Most of the members of the medical professions come from the middle class and retain attitudes compatibile with the shrinking middle class. Those in the higher and lower socio-economic classes, divergent from our usual focus may be difficult, demanding, and unreliable and consume inordinate time and energy in dealing with them in medical encounters. Yet, these trends have occurred in a brief period of time. The middle class is likely to continue to shrink, placing a greater strain on healthcare professions and medical facilities.

Consequently, an awareness of these trends to the functioning of medical services, as well as other community services and businesses, becomes essential.

I wish to emphasize that these behavior categories are very broad and only represent generalizations from experience. We have many people in the higher and lower brands that are wonderful, stimulating and inspiring in their daily lives when touched by illness and adversity in their families. By the same token, the middle brand is no guarantee of absence of the behaviors cited. Under the stress of personal tragedy, personal or family illness, nearly everyone experiences a departure from normal, controlled, civilized behavior in some manner and to some degree. We must be prepared for it. People tend to reciprocate how they are treated–kindness with kindness, anger with anger. Medical professionals cannot, must not react in kind to those with serious personal tribulations but maintain a professional demeanor and understanding.

D. THE SOCIO-ECONOMICALLY ADVANTAGED OR *THE SICK-SYBARITE SYNDROME*

> "I don't really like attending such people so well as the poor. The cases are more monotonous, and one has to go through more fuss and listen more deferentially to nonsense."
>
> Dr. Tertius Lydgate, *Middlemarch* (1872), George Eliot.

The Sick-Sybarite Syndrome acquired its name from the citizens of the ancient Greek city of Sybara in southern Italy noted for its mild climate, fine food and drink, and ease of living. The Sybarite, devoted to luxury and sensuous pleasure made possible by affluence, can be defined by terms of trendy, chic, yuppie, upscale, high-maintenance, etc. Appearance of health, fashionable design, and a sense of style take precedence over needs, taxing budgets by struggling towards the appearances of greater affluence. Wants become needs; as Noel Coward aptly said, "Give us the luxuries of life and to hell with necessities."

The socio-economically advantaged Sybarite exhibits the 'Vuitton sign'—graded one to ten by the number of pieces of Vuitton luggage looped over the forearm, a sloppy hobo or career shopper or duffle sac or sheri mule or cargo bag–Fendi, Ferragamo, Prada–they blur together. Or the 'Coordinated Sign,' or the 'I've-got-it-all Sign.' Materially in command of themselves, they may be sweetly confrontational. The Sign of Louis Vuitton may herald the truly hostile and distrustful:

A medical paraprofessional from out of town, husband a highly paid professional, visited her father in the hospital. Along with a platter or cornucopia of affluence and chic uselessness, on each arm were three large Louis Vuitton carrying-bags and a couple of others draped here and there. They couldn't have had much in them or she would have been weighted down. Much display about where she should put them and alluding to how much trouble and responsibility the bags were when she traveled at the beginning of each conversation drew attention to the Sybarite, but such inconvenience be must endured.

She arrived at the hospital early each morning sporting a different, colorful and stylish outfit, going into the nurses station to show her wares and to lord it over those who merely worked. Preening and prinking before the mirror, she set things just right, but not for long because such paraphernalia requires constant attention with repeated adjustment and patting back into place. Our Sybarite is certainly part of the idle, game-shooting privileged class noted by Thomas Carlyle and his "Gospel of Dilettantism" or "Mammonism" which, at least, worked. He writes, "'Make money' that will mean withal, 'Do work in order to make money.' But, 'Go gracefully idle in Mayfair'"[2] London's most fashionable quarter. Appearance of affluence and fluff was everything.

Sybarites live in an artificial, hierarchical world of corporate or professional structures where the importance of superficial and singular impressions are paramount, often moving from place to place, from job to job, and marriage to marriage. Though insecure in their professional lives and personal lives, they must manifest an air of control and mastery, appearing *on-top-of-the-world*. Don't expect to see warmth or human kindness in the event of a health crisis. Narcissistic and self-centered to the core, the Sybarite's impersonal world of the professions and corporations interferes with creating a lasting physician-patient relationship. Manipulation is their key to success: cold and distrustful while appearing to be gracious and personable.

Today, the Sybarite lives in what C.S. Lewis called the 'Managerial Age' where the greatest evil occurs in sordid "dens of crime," conceived and ordered, moved and seconded, carried and minuted in clean, carpeted, well-lighted offices by quiet men and women, who do not raise their voices: "Everyone wishes everyone else's discrediting, demotion, and ruin; everyone is an expert in the confidential report, the pretended alliance, the stab in the back. Overall this their good manners, their expressions of grave respect, their 'tributes' to one another's invaluable services form a thin crust. Every now and then it gets punctured, and the scalding lava of their hatred spurts out."[3] An atmosphere of the purest distrust.

Everything revolves about the Sybarites' time and schedule with many cancelled or missed appointments. They expect 'special' favors and 'special' attention, ask many questions of little relevance, with a *me* focus, saying they can't be inconvenienced while inconveniencing others. Sybarites are manipulative, the ultimate control freaks, objecting to most attempts at possible solutions, with an unwillingness to participate if it interferes with their sense of style or seeking pleasures, their presence made known by the cellular telephone, talking loudly, interfering with others' concentration.

Above all, the Sybarite must make a good impression, or at least appear exceptional, even if obnoxious. And they don't tolerate being inconvenienced by

---

[2] Thomas Carlyle. *Past and Present* (1843) editor Richard Altick. New York: New York University Press, 1965, p. 152.
[3] C.S. Lewis. *The Screwtape Letters*. 28th printing. New York: Macmillan, 1980, p. x-xi.

illness, theirs or anyone else's. With a blizzard of empty, wingy questions, Sybarites keeps the staff on the defensive by asking an excessive number of questions that go far beyond requests for reasonable and necessary information. "Who ever asks the questions has control," says the Sybarite, and it's control the Sybarite wants, and it's control of the Sybarite that the medical staff must establish.

The Sybarites arrive for appointments fashionably late, often attired in their *toga virilis* of tennis or golf outfits, showing great difficulty accepting the annoyance of illness, especially other peoples' woes, not wanting to allow anything to interfere with pursuit of pleasure and self-interest: "I want to get on with *my* life" i.e., it is not convenient to be sick, to take medicine, follow instructions, or keep appointments. Some Sybarites exhibit a sense of guilt about their self-interest, while with most sick-Sybarites, self-interest knows no bounds.

Sybarites expect lengthy, detailed explanations, but give the impression of being indifferent while adjusting their designer garments or ostentatious jewelry while studying themselves in a mirror. Exasperating by practice, they turn medical personnel against each other, which is an especially difficult delay tactic as discharge from the hospital approaches since they must assume responsibility for themselves or for someone else: the patient. On eve of discharge from the hospital, expect further objections about inconvenience to themselves and occasionally a refusal to become involved even if the patient is their spouse or parent. Strangely, a vacation has been scheduled that interferes with discharge plans.

If the Sybarite is not recognized, the staff may become divided and work at cross purposes. If behavior gets out of hand, the staff tends to avoid the Sybarite. The staff may expect too much of Sybarites because they appear successful in other areas, but Sybarites may be incompetent in the simplest, basic elements of human behavior. By setting up the staff for failure if their every wish and whim is not satisfied, they are quick to express disappointment and distrust, under-cutting confidence and trust in the medical staff. An uncontrolled Sybarite can be disruptive to the care of patients and disruptive to functioning of the therapy staff and Rehabilitation Unit. The staff may become defensive or angry and lash out at the Sybarite, which confirms to the Sybarite that their distrust is justified. Managing the Sybarite may take an inordinate amount of time, energy, and resources if the staff is not prepared.

A "Pre-morbid" sick-Sybarite devotes a great part of himself or herself to health consciousness evoking a manner of superiority in healthy-chic, a paradigm of style. Survival is everything, for Sybarites expect to be around to spend their money—all of it. They absorb articles in health magazines, newspapers and women's and men's fashion magazines, bring clippings to the doctor as a point of argument. While thinking nothing of spending the better part of a day searching after shallots or goat cheese, the Sybarite will not lightly suffer inconvenience of waiting for a doctor or appointments at the laboratory or X-ray office. Sybarites readily develop a credulous enthusiasm for the latest anti-establishment, counter-culture, health marketed scheme: the medical and economic consequences are considerable. Rarely does the Sybarite express gratitude. Some may be distrustful and overbearing, and attempt to bully the staff, making accusations about lapses in care, and they go to administration or the Quality Assurance Office, or other authority with little hesitation.

The 'pre-morbid' sick-Sybarite, steeped in a little knowledge, becomes a self-appointed amateur physician with one devoted patient, verifying an ancient medical truth: the doctor who treats himself has a fool for a doctor and a fool for a patient. The Sybarite, though quick to offer medical advice to others, is quicker to deny responsibility and shifts responsibility to others. Notorious for slow pay, complaints and quibbling about fees are perceived as stylish, chic. In spite of financial advantages, the sick-Sybarite is predictably slow in sending forms to their insurance company, and haggles interminably with the bookkeeper over the smallest of details.

The sick-Sybarite lives under time-pressure and contacts tend to be urgent, with a mastery of the drop-in visit. They may regard the doctor's office or hospital in a mechanistic view as the "fix-it shop," like taking the kids to the hair stylist or the dog to be clipped. Rudeness and condescension to the office staff and nurses is *de rigueur*. They force their way in to the inner office, and manipulate the doctor against the staff with a negative effect on office morale.

Nevertheless, Sybarites fall prey to the same ills as everyone else, as if the occurrence of illness manifests the commonality of man. Good fortune and tragedy keep close company. We might expect a sick-Sybarite to react in a manner different from other patients. Vague symptoms may prompt a visit to their primary doctor, but small complaints prompt consultation with a specialist and a second opinion or two. The sick-Sybarite engages the physician with a commingling of haughtiness and terror. Consequently, when the Sybarite becomes sick, i.e. a 'morbid sick-Sybarite,' the reaction is not an honest, straight-forward description of symptoms or a forthright appeal for relief, but a round-about, circular contest of wills.

The sick-Sybarite, adept at the art of irrelevant, repetitive, mincing questions, is able to brabble any subject to death without gaining understanding. A simple, logical explanation or the actual imparting of information leads to dissatisfaction, while the use of jargon, especially multiple, polysyllabic words not intended for clarity, are received with as much satisfaction as the sick-Sybarite is able to muster. They do not ask the doctor to explain a medically arcane phrases. If the questions have any common thread, they lead to demand for prediction of the future, and lack of a definitive answer is used as reason for distrust, for he or she feels deceived by the odds or chances which, in the Sybarite's view, should be overwhelmingly in their favor. Be especially wary of the "why -question," which is *not* a request for information, but is a complaint or an attack that prompts a defensive response.

Lack of trust, or distrust, becomes the major impediment in dealing with the sick-Sybarite and the establishment of a workable physician-patient relationship. Their *modus vivendi* is "trust no one," certainly not doctors or medical professionals in general. The sick-Sybarite demands second opinions, and third and fourth, expressing satisfaction if opinions differ, which is sometimes the case since no two of a trade agree.

The 'benign' sick-Sybarite may eventually accept the reality of their situation and expose an underlying good nature, distorted by affluence, but when faced with a difficult medical problem, rallies in a mature manner. They may even develop a human quality, although such a conversion is not often observed. Relapse to the Sybaritic style on recovery, however, is the norm. On the other hand, the 'malignant' sick-Sybarite displays an intense ill-will: "As if forced by fate to eat black bread themselves, make certain others partake of their fare."[4] The aging sick-Sybarite does not change, but behaves in the same manner as in earlier Sybaritic periods of life. Don't expect growth or a new awareness.

Impossible to satisfy, the physician may harbor a feeling of guilt or failure when a Sybarite switches to a new doctor, when in fact, the Sybarite is doing what Sybarites do. Yesterday's doctor is tarred with the same brush as a dispatched clothing designer, discarded high-tech tennis racket, or last degraded health food. In spite of best efforts of physicians to understand and treat sick-Sybarites, Sybarites have a remarkable way of summarily dismissing their physician to seek care elsewhere, enacting the same scene.

The physician who receives the sick-Sybarite from another physician must be on guard because the sick-Sybarite initially appears personable and flatters the new physician while coyly criticizing the old, and in the process, sets up the new physician. In the transient world of the Sybarite, the doctor who displays a concern for the care of and loyalty to 'my' patients–the sick-Sybarite–is often crest-fallen and disillusioned to find 'my' patient's loyalty belongs to the

---

[4] Herman Melville. "Benito Cereno" (1855) *Selected Writings of Herman Melville*. New York: Modern Library, 1952.

Sybarite's unstable insurance plan. The sick-Sybarite adeptly manipulates systems of large HMOs, IPAs, and similar organizations, and side-stepping "gatekeepers" is their specialty. The sick-Sybarite over-matches their attempts to limit access, for working through intricacies of complex barriers is what Sybarites do best.

The sick-Sybarite crosses many personality types. Since they have witnessed the deadly sin of Lust downgraded, declassified, transliterated, and transmogrified into recreation or nuisance, the sick Sybarite perceives the Other Six can be practiced with abandon: Pride, Covetousness, Anger, Gluttony, Envy, and Sloth in pursuing sensuous pleasure and indolent leisure. If the sick-Sybarite accepts a religious faith, he or she appeals to the Almighty for the continuance of material favors and pleasures. More than once I have heard, "I believe in God [depending on which one is *au courant*] and I shouldn't have to deal with this." Adding, "And I want something done about it!" Even more disillusioning is the 'morbidly sick-Sybarite' who seeks to the ends of the earth for a cure, and failing, seeks revenge on the healthy and against the medical professional.

In their manner of coping with illness, the Sybarite is appallingly similar to the Medicaid patient or the socio-economically *disadvantaged*. Gaining their trust is essential, and at the same time, a monumental, exasperating task. Explanations must be impressive, and it is best to use a healthy amount of technical terms and jargon which makes the Sybarite feel that you have taken them into your confidence. They will never ask for an explanation of technical words or concepts they don't and can't possibly understand; they cannot allow the impression that they don't know.

With constraints placed on physicians by Medicare and the insurance industry, elderly, affluent sick-Sybarites, with their myriad of complaints and blizzard of airy questions who appear with their angry, impatient off-spring with their objections and notes on yellow tablets, find themselves *persona non grata* when down to earth patients who have the same problems present themselves to the physician more directly and honestly, are reimbursed at the same rate.

Although management of sick-Sybarites is important in an affluent society, the economic impact of sick-Sybarites in national health is enormous. Since medical expenses of the sick-Sybarites are largely paid by company insurance, no price is too great, as long as it does not come from the Sybarite's own pocket or detract from their sense of style or consumption of pleasures.

Working the system, competitiveness, self-interest in a shifting, uncertain pecking order in an over-socialized, primitive behavior resides the Sybarite. Often devoid of substance, the Sybarite lives on credit. Gullible to fads and fashions of health matters, Sybarites are easy prey for the 'feel-good' trade, alternative medicine promoters, and readily, eagerly went into fancies like managed care.

They may appear to be friendly and an ally, or on equal footing with the medical staff, but they do not reciprocate. Gently, but persistently engage them in some aspect of care. Make them responsible for the simplest duty. Keeping them engaged is of utmost importance. The staff must maintain consistency in managing the Sybarite, because the slightest inconsistency is magnified into gross error and distrust.

In the case of anothers' illness, one question that sets the Sybarite on red-alert is, "Is it contagious?" If negative, a sigh and resumption of their prior self-absorbed state follows.

How to deal with them runs counter or opposite to what the ethicists, lawyers, etc. say: the medical staff must take charge, take the initiative and wrest control away from the Sybarite. Give explanations to them in maximum technical language, and wait. Don't explain. They will not ask for clarification, but they will consider that their egos have been flattered by being taken into the doctor's confidence. Explanations should be direct, to the point, and avoid repetition of the same material or the same explanations. If they demand an explanation that has already been covered and explained, respond, "We have covered that matter, what don't you understand?" Written instructions are helpful, especially if on official stationery with designer logo, names of heads of departments, etc.

If a Sybarite takes a threatening, suspicious tack, the staff can diminish this behavior by explaining the simplest procedures as they are performed, such as describing the medicines when brought, or the diet, or what therapy is intended to accomplish. Keep it brief, down-to-earth, specific and spiced with medical terms.

In the case that trust is established, keep your distance. Best not to become overly involved with their family, associates, careers, interests, etc. at the time of medical contact. They often appear to lead glamorous or exciting lives, but at base, they are desperate and struggling while submerging fears and anxieties, which only come out during irrational explosions of rage. Maintain an objective, fiduciary relationship—cordial, but business-like, ever cautious not to get caught-up in their trappings of affluence.

Above all, don't expect gratitude, don't expect an expression of trust. The Sybarites may behave in a manner more consistent with the disadvantaged at times, especially if their socio-economic background is one of being disadvantaged in earlier times.

E. THE DISADVANTAGED, MEDICAID

"Why should the poor be flattered?" *Hamlet* 3.2.55.

Life in the streets. Life in jail. Life on the lamb. Life sleeping in parks. Our Trauma Service brings a steady population of the socio-economically disadvantaged. Some have been beaten or shot in drug dealing. If adolescent, their parents are sometimes on drugs or in jail. They live in a cross-reality of alleyways, hideouts, boxcars, and porches. Double-dealing is the norm. Out of the main stream–way out of the main stream–these disadvantaged patients live by their wits and luck, mostly bad. The hierarchical social welfare system is often the hierarchy of the streets. Only the immediate and present exist. No time for abstract notions of other places and other ways. The visible is only part of the threat of daily life. What is not seen may be equally fearsome. Anything or anyone not already known is suspect, not trusted. Life in the raw, nuts and bolts reality.

The Medi-caid, disadvantaged, and unsophisticated patient, especially if on welfare, may present a particularly difficult problem of management. In the hospital, they are in a strange and bewildering, unfamiliar environment: clean sheets, soap and water, towels, slippers, warm food–all threatening under the circumstances. Many have struggled to cope with a welfare bureaucracy that may be unsympathetic and mysterious to many of these patients. Others have spent so much time coping with the welfare or penal system, they know it inside and out.

The principle difficulty in dealing effectively with these disadvantaged patients is gaining their trust because the welfare system and their daily existence is based on distrust and watching out for one's self. Gaining trust is especially difficult because they do not understand the complex language they hear and circumstances they are in while in the hospital. Consequently, they may become suspicious, distant, and uncooperative. The patients may call out to the staff instead of using the call-light or other ordinary means of communication demanding whatever they need to be delivered immediately. Their behavior may escalate into threatening and vulgar language jeopardizing communications with other patients and families.

Sullen. Flat affect. No eye contact, or a threatening stare. Monosyllabic, terse speech. Completely in the present. This is no time for warm, professionally sincere, friendly greetings; not a time to get up-close to their face, an ingratiating smile, a meaningful clasp of the hand, and looking deep into their eyes, and say, "How are you?" "Did you sleep well?" "Did you have a bowel movement?"

The staff may begin to perceive the disadvantaged patient as sub-human or behold them as animalistic, and reciprocate their inconsideration with more inconsideration or openly insulting behavior to match that of the disadvantaged patient. Rather than building trust, a widening gulf develops that hampers effective communication and cooperation between patient and staff. The patient calls for the nurse or doctor by loudly calling, "Hey!" or "Hey, you!" which is a clue, already obvious, to the type of behavior that must be dealt with. Staff and physicians may be compared between other disadvantaged patients in openly disparaging terms, and within hearing of other patients and families. Disruptive outbursts may cause the entire nursing floor or ward to be disturbed.

Constant contact with an over-worked and under-funded welfare system, long waits, and inconsistent responsiveness by the social system inhibits what social interaction these patients and their families are capable of so that they become wary of all strangers and any question. They behave and interact by a different code of behavior than the rest of society, and should not be expected to show the same courtesies or graces of middle class health care workers. All of these social acts are threatening to someone who comes from the streets and drug hangouts. Also, these individuals are sometimes dangerous, they are more likely to swing a fist or elbow than to respond with an agreeable social response.

In dealing with the socio-economically disadvantaged, *don't say hello, don't say goodbye.*

When entering the room, do *not* say "good morning" and when leaving their room do *not* say "goodbye." At least initially, do not use ordinary social greetings that the disadvantaged patient might consider off-putting or insulting. After some time, when the patient is more secure, such greetings and salutations may be appropriate. Even simple questions such as inquiries about their children may be perceived as meddling and best reserved until rapport and trust have been established. By not using salutations that are outside the customs of the disadvantaged patient, omitting this part of conversation and going directly to what ever is to be done, the patient feels that he or she is being treated as an equal in a less threatening manner.

Rather than social, well-meaning friendliness, a matter-of-fact manner is best at the beginning: touch or move something before saying *anything*. The bedstead. Bedside table. Adjust the bedcovers. Look at a toe. You are telling them that you are in charge in a non-threatening way. Give a simple instruction: "stick out your tongue," or "hold your hands like this." A command so simple that it carries no meaning. Do your examination. Ask only pertinent questions with no commentary. No chatter. No socialization. Always with respect.

When you are ready to leave the room—leave! Do not say "goodbye," or "I'll see you tomorrow," or "Have a great day." Leave. Once you have decided to leave the room, turn to the door and—go. No matter what might be said that could detain you, don't stop until you are out of sight. If necessary, return to respond to a question, but leave first.

Do not respond to "Hey!" called to you from the patient's room when you are passing in the hallway. If they persist, instruct them that your name is Dr. __ and when they refer to you correctly, you will return. The first time you hold the line is the hardest, and each time after will be difficult, but management of the patient may rest on how well this first interaction is carried out.

Various ethnic groups behave somewhat differently, but some general principles apply. Gaining the disadvantaged patient's trust is the primary goal, but requires slightly different manners. Explain in the simplest terms just what you expect of them and what you are doing, such as what the medicines are and what they do. Do not use jargon or technical language. Explaining that a medicine is for blood pressure, or diabetes, or heart medicine is enough. But saying that a medicine is a beta-blocker, or hypoglycemic agent, or anti-arrhythmic medicine is not appropriate because the patient might think you are talking down to them or insulting their intelligence. Slowly gain their trust, then explain in more detail, or educate. But not at the first encounters.

Once the disadvantaged patient gets to know who you are and who is in charge, and it is you and not them, a remarkable transformation may occur. I say *may* occur, or may not occur. One never knows, but many socio-economically disadvantaged individuals show an astonishing growth and development, especially while in a secure and structured environment of the hospital. But you, the doctor and medical professionals, must establish the structure and their expected behavior. The willingness of the disadvantaged to toe-the-line can be amazing, and at times disconcerting. And in their own way, they may express gratitude, mainly by cooperating, or by bringing a mess of fish or a basket of corn, but not the usual expressions of gratitude.

F. MOM'S LIST

Some time after the incident at the beginning of this chapter, the mother of a hospitalized patient came to my office for a conference. The patient was in her mid-twenties with a very serious illness. The mother had a yellow tablet of questions prepared. She was quiet, composed, and polite.

I patiently answered each of her questions as thoroughly as possible, making certain that I explained the medical findings in terms that she would understand and inquiring if further explanation was needed. I noticed as she turned from one page of questions to the next, that she seemed not be listening to my answers as much as noting how I responded and how confident I was of my diagnoses and management. I followed the protocol of full disclosure with permission of her daughter, the patient. As we went on, I grew bolder, using more technical language and explanation than before. Some I was sure she didn't understand at first but she did not ask questions. In the case of complex matters, I made certain that my explanations were as clear as possible.

After each of her questions had been dealt with, she left the office in the same assured, confident and considerate manner. From that time on, both the patient and family have been most loyal and trusting of my care and judgement.

Again, I don't think the information conveyed was as important as the face to face meeting and non-verbal communication. She concluded that she could trust my care of her daughter, and that I would keep her informed of progress. Many difficult times followed, but the patient and family followed my advice. Now, more than a decade later, we are still patient and physician and, I add, friend and friend.

Establishing trust at the beginning of our physician-patient relationship was the cornerstone of management. In other instances, the initial interview did not go as well and the patient and family either became suspicious or moved on to another doctor. Although for some physicians, the loss of a patient to another doctor is a threat, such as chronicled by Anthony Trollope in *Doctor Thorne* (1858) and the peoples of Barsetshire, is a blow to one's ego and professional pride. However, a doctor cannot be all things to all people; and in the case of distrust, both parties are better served if a relationship of trust is either established in time or the relationship is ended by either party. Strong medicine for the new physician, but a wise potion for the experienced.

G. SIGN OF THE YELLOW TABLET

Patients and families come to the office or meetings with a variety of recording devices, such as tape recorders and tablets. So far, no one has used a video recorder, but I'm waiting. Most bring some sort of paper for note taking, and many arrive with their yellow tablets. The presence of a yellow tablet may be a warning or simply off-putting, depending on the intent of the holder of the tablet.

The yellow tablet serves many purposes in addition to taking notes or obtaining information. Yellow tablets come in various sizes with associated connotations. The 5 X 7 inch tablets are for the inexperienced and benign. These tablets carry little threat and the questions tend to be limited, as if the note-taker doesn't expect to ask many questions or to take down much information. Family members carry these tablets in a purse or small paper bag with a store logo, and are mainly for limited shopping lists, notes to the gardener, or directions to a store or social meeting. If questions are recorded, they tend to be brief and either irrelevant or vague. A certain disorganization usually accompanies the small yellow tablets, with apologies and combined with a measure of fluster about what to ask and what is important. In this case, the staff should not be put-off by the yellow tablet, but use this as an opportunity to educate, guide, and reassure. Often the small yellow tablet is put away mid-way through a family conference, and the business of the meeting proceeds.

Yellow tablets 8½ x 11 inches also tend to be benign, but a little more serious and business-like than the 5 x 7 inch tablets. Sometimes 8½ x 11 tablets contain extensive lists of prepared questions and provide adequate space for taking notes, sometimes space for extensive notes. With a little ceremony, the tablets are slowly withdrawn, often with an apology for the necessity to take notes or that details are often lost or forgotten. A few people arrive with pages and pages of questions and need for detail, and at the same time, tend to be reasonable. Family members who need information for discharge arrangements, medications, etc. may benefit from such record keeping. Pages are turned with a certain fluster and lack of purpose, as if to say, 'this is very difficult for me.' So, take note and make the family member at ease as much as possible. Readily provide them with whatever information and details they may require. It is an opportunity to gain trust and earn the family's gratitude.

The tablet size 8½ x 14 inches is a different matter. These tablet-carriers may be out to intimidate, to cause harm, to threaten, and most of all, to destroy trust. Carriers of these tablets make every display that they carry a 'legal' tablet, that it implies a legal sanction, if not a legal threat. They bring their legal yellow tablets into the office with much commotion, demonstration and pompousness, usually in a new brief case or leather folder. Sitting in the chair next to the physician's desk, they spread out their bags and papers while opening the yellow tablet to a prepared, correct page. The tablet is turned so that the doctor can see the many questions written, underlined and starred.

The pen, too, is a give-away. If it is pink or a shiny gold or silver plastic pen, or a Mickey Mouse design, the serious effect they mean to create is largely destroyed. If it is an expensive collector or corporate pen like a gold and burgundy emblazoned Aurora or silver celebrity Mont Blanc, it's over-kill, and the intimidating effect is blunted or lost. If a pencil is used, more likely it is a stubby Ticonderoga No. 2 that won't last through any lengthy interrogation, which is the implied purpose of the 8½ x 14 yellow tablet. The serious, untrusting, business-like use a black, serious, untrusting pen that will write under water or in outer space, and will not run out of ink.

Nevertheless, the carriers of the larger 8½ x 14 inch yellow tablets may be in a malignant frame of mind when they purchased the tablet at a drug store or cut rate office supply store, or they may be merely malignant and untrusting. The legal yellow tablet says that judge and jury are not necessary, they will dish out their own style of oppressive justice if they deem necessary. No matter what, if they can make those interviewed uncomfortable or restless, a measure of frontier justice has been achieved.

In the end, the legal tablet generally signals a puffer or windbag. These pretenders to the bar are not out on a mission to show the goodness of human nature or the nutritive value of the milk of human kindness, but to undermine trust, and make sure that the doctor knows about it and that they mean business, more or less, although in all likelihood, they have no idea of what business they intend except to make a pest of themselves. In one instance, husband and wife arrived with matching 'legal' size tablets, but could not agree on what questions to ask, and their show of force was weakened.

Nevertheless, the legal yellow tablet rates status as a type of warning. Warning that they are going to take as much of your time and energy as you will allow. Trust or its development are not on their agenda. Gaining trust may be difficult under the Sign of the Yellow Tablet, but take their comments and questions seriously. In the end, treating their yellow tablet-questions as complaints and not so much as questions gives the doctor an advantage, but an encounter with a yellow tablet, legal size, must be handled carefully. Occasionally, it is a chance to clarify difficult problems or to settle differences of opinion, but in my experience, the 'legal' tablet heralds and records distrust in heavy measure. The yellow, bright, glaring, attention-calling pads are not to be trifled with, but the wary cautioned to negotiate yellow tablet-carriers carefully and skillfully. It is not a time for social conversation, but matter-of-fact direct facing issues without illusion.

A few family members bring tablets that may be in any of the three sizes that have a low-glare gray tone that is easy on the eye. These tablet-carriers are welcomed with gladness and good humor. Most likely, they are trustful, and can be trusted to follow through with medical recommendations and future plans.

Chapter 2

COMPLAINTS

A. THE COMPLAINER

The complainer is one of the most valuable and, at the same time, one of the most annoying and troublesome persons to deal with in a therapeutic setting. The individual who complains may be an asset in disguise because if something is actually wrong or not properly attended to, the physician and therapy team need to know about it. Therefore, listening to the complaint is most important since the complaint may provide consequential and imperative information. You may not become aware of something amiss until someone complains about it, consequently, acknowledge the complaint at once and allow that the complaint may be valid.

However, some complainers go far beyond what is reasonable or useful in the manner and nature of their complaint. Their complaints are more a matter of habit, or coping style, or natural disposition. These are the complainers who are difficult to manage and must be recognized early on. Your suspicion may be corroborated by asking someone acquainted with the complainer if complaining is ordinary or typical behavior for this individual. Usually, emphatic agreement follows by the acquaintance who says that a complaining-style is, in fact, the norm for this person.

Once acknowledgement is obtained, the shift of control should go to the physician and therapy team if handled carefully.

Some complainers regard nothing too small or too trivial not to complain about. To the complainer, everything is terrible until perfect. Often, the complaint is irrelevant to the medical circumstances or to important considerations for the patient's care, lending a degree of illogic to the complaint. The complaint may even seem to misdirect attention from matters-at-hand. The complainer assumes an attitude of helplessness and absurdity along with their dissatisfaction and distrust.

The complainer may be regarded as a pest by the therapy team, taking up time and energy on trivial considerations, resulting in annoyance and, in private, express anger toward the complainer. The usual reaction of the staff is irritation and impatience which may lead to avoidance and inattention toward the complainer or the patient, which tends to validate the complainer's complaint to himself or herself. If the complainer remains in a therapeutic situation for an extended period of time, such as a long hospitalization, the staff may express overt hostility toward the complainer and disregard their complaints.

Though the complainer may be vocal and forceful, occasionally appearing angry and threatening, in fact, the complainer feels helpless and out of control. By complaining, the complainer relieves himself or herself of responsibility. Once he has pointed out his complaint and expressed his dissatisfaction, the complainer is free of anxiety and responsibility because he or she has made the helper responsible for making the complainer feel better: a behavior that irritates therapy staff unless recognized as a statement of helplessness.

Although the staff may be put off by the complainer, the most important step in managing the complainer is to listen to the complaint without passing judgement, which is much easier if done at the first interaction rather than after the situation becomes complicated by negative attitudes toward the complainer and escalated into a hostile confrontation.

The success or failure of management of the entire case may depend on how well a complaint and the complainer is handled. If the complainer is handled with respect and in a non-confrontational way, a distressing, time-consuming, and potentially disastrous situation may be turned into a therapeutic advantage. It may be difficult to imagine, but the complainer who has been treated with respect and courtesy may become an equally vocal advocate for the staff and institution once their complaint has been satisfied.

If the complainer is allowed to get out of control, the complainer may undermine all therapeutic efforts. Complaints follow on complaints until the staff is inundated and exasperated by their complaints and the needs of one individual or complainer. Complaints tend to escalate to the point that no one can defuse them and the complainer takes their grievances to higher and higher administrative positions.

The worst outcome of an uncontrolled complainer's distrustfulness is divisiveness of the staff about who is to take care of the patient and who must deal with the complainer. The complaints, even if important and valid, may be disregarded and ignored by the staff which rapidly aggravates an already difficult situation into a potentially dangerous one.

Early recognition and intervention saves endless aggravation and preserves the trust of patient and family. It is never easy, but dealing with the complaint (and the complaint only and not the negative affect of the complainer) without judgement of the complainer removes the emotive aspect of the complaint, often the complaint carries with it information that you most need to know.

B. THE COMPLAINT[1]

A complaint usually arises from an expectation that was not met. The complaint may be valuable in that the complainer usually has a point. Listening to the complaint when we are least inclined to do so becomes essential. If no one complains, we may think that all is well, the logical error of *argumentum ad quietem* or, *the quietist, or "no complaint,"* if nobody complains, nobody suffers.[2]

The most common reasons why people complain are an unrelated event, something not explained well, unjust or unfair treatment, something seems ridiculous, something malfunctioned, a promise wasn't kept, they are mentally or physically ill, they feel they are getting the run around, or someone is rude, indifferent or discourteous.

Most people don't want to complain, so when a person complains, by all means, listen to them. Sometimes, listening to what they have to say is all that is needed. That their concerns are being taken seriously can make a great difference in future dealings with the patient and family. The complaint may tell us something we very much need to know. In that case, thank them for the complaint, that is, for the information.

The difference between a *complaint* and the *complainer* is the difference between being *upset* and being plain *difficult*. When upset, the individual complains to bring something amiss to our attention because they perceive we are in a position to do something about it. In this sense, a complaint is a backhanded compliment. These people are often ill-at-ease in making a complaint because it is not part of their normal manner. In this instance, their complaint may sound particularly offensive because they are not skilled in bringing complaints to the attention of others.

---

[1] Maudelle Terry. April 5, 2001. With permission.
[2] Jeremy Bentham. *Bentham's Book of Political Fallacies*. editor Harold A. Larrabee. Baltimore: The Johns Hopkins Press, 1952.

When a difficult person demands attention, they enjoy being disruptive and negative causing distress in others. They are highly skilled and practiced in making complaints. Their complaints are articulate, smooth, and to the point. Little emotion may be evident, but a detached and observing stance, watching for reaction and what effect their complaint is having on the recipient of the complaint. Communicating with them is often frustrating and occasionally impossible. No single method is effective in all situations. Nevertheless, the complaints can be dealt with in the same manner in either case.

Listen to the complaint. Ask for specifics. Get details. Complaints may be vague and diffuse, but you must get the information before you can resolve a complaint. If necessary, take notes and read them back to the complainer. Ask that he or she verify the details and specifics of the complaint. If the complaint contains abusive and insulting language, write down the exact words. Read the complaint back to the complainer, and sometimes the hyperbole of the complaint and exaggerations will be modified or withdrawn.

More than anything, showing interest in the complainer and his or her complaint is one of the most effective elements in easing the behavior of the complainer before it gets out of control. If the complaint is demeaned or disregarded, the complainer feels undermined or abandoned, but taking a complaint seriously, even if wholly absurd, often serves to establish trust. If you take an absurd complaint seriously, they can trust that you will take an important complaint equally seriously.

Apologize. "I'm sorry that happened, —to hear that, —for the misunderstanding." And respond to their complaints with, "I see," "I understand." Even if you know that the complaint is not important and even if it is not true, an apology tends to defuse the thrust of the complaint and does not weaken the position of the therapy staff. Apologizing to the angry complainer may be onerous at first, but the change in their attitude is often remarkable and reassuring. By all means, avoid statements like, "That's not important" which tends to stiffen the complainer's will to make trouble. An apology validates the complainer's concern and keeps the responsibility on the complainer. Many physicians and members of the medical staff refuse to apologize, considering it a sign of weakness or giving in or as an attack on their authority or ego or pride.

Listening to the complaint and apologizing for the inconvenience or discomfort or confusion is often all that is required. If the complainer is not satisfied, tell the complainer that you will look into the matter and that you will respond at a specific time–on *your* terms and not the complainer's terms. Check on the validity of the complaint and respond in writing or by meeting at a particular time. If your inquiry shows that the complaint was in fact valid, tell the complainer so and thank him or her for bringing the matter to your attention. If the complaint is not valid, inform the complainer in matter-of-fact, unemotional terms that you were unable to verify their complaint. Possibly an alternative explanation will satisfy the complaint. It does no harm to thank the complainer for their interest or calling attention to what they thought amiss, even though your instincts may direct you otherwise, that you may want to show the complainer up by refutation of the complaint. At this time, maintaining a professional manner helps to diffuse the complaint.

Confront a difficult, complaining individual exuding confidence; you must be an actor at this time. They look for your weaknesses and zero in on them if you allow. Stand up if you are seated when they enter room. Take control in no uncertain terms. "How can I help you?"

Use positive language. Never say "you," say "We must," "Let's do this."

Avoid "you should have," "or I can't." Instead, say "let's see."

Do not say, "It's impossible," rather "Let's explore some options."

Preferable to "if" is to say, "when we…"

"I don't know…" can be changed to, "Let me check."

"But…" is not as effective as saying, "However…" which is more positive.

Have pencil and paper ready when confronting a difficult, complaining person. Interrupt once, after about 10 to 15 seconds, to check something.

Ask a question you already know the answer to. Write down their exaggerations, and say, "I'm writing this down," if especially the confrontation is over the telephone.

Make non-committal statements, no promises. "I'm sorry you feel that way." "We try our best."

With any complaint, *skip the blame, solve the problem*. Every member of the therapy staff must work together. Don't let blame to be directed onto other workers.

Restate the complaint in their words: "Do I have your concerns right?" And be certain to follow-up on the complaint.

The therapy team must have an escape plan. Teamwork is essential. Don't allow the difficult person to divide and antagonize the staff. If necessary, include Security. Develop a code for difficult people. Start a *Most Wanted List*. Do not tolerate abuse. Politely use repetition of "we": "We are not here to take abuse." Expect the complainer to behave as an adult. Remember that you, too, are an adult; *no* crying. No hysterics. No fawning and groveling before the complainer.

In the case of an out of control or insulting, abusive, complaining individual, say, "When can we talk as adults?" or "I suggest we talk when you are under control."

Take control, you are in charge. You are the only one who can make a difference. You are the only one who can satisfy or defuse the complaint and the complainer. Your body language must be positive, no shrinking violet. Sit erect. Stand erect. Strong voice, deep and firm, no squeaks.

In business, 96 per cent of dissatisfied customers do not complain about something they don't like, however the average dissatisfied customer tells ten people about their dissatisfying experience. On the other hand, ninety-five per cent of those whose complaints are resolved continue to do business with the same company, and on average, they tell five people of their more positive experience. Thus, resolving complaints not only aids in taking care of a sometimes unknown problem, doing so also gains or maintains the trust of the patient and family. Taking the time and effort to resolve a justified complaint yields rich benefits to all parties.

C. THE ANGRY, UPSET COMPLAINER

The angry, upset complainer may present an opportunity to score big. To the angry complainer, everything is wrong, until everything is right. No service, appointment time, or nuance of therapy is above being criticized, and the focus of a complaint. One complaint tends to generate more and more complaints: Everything is wrong. Everyone is terrible. No one is in charge. No one is helping them. No one cares.

The angry, upset complainer may affect disgust and threat when, in fact, most are fairly benign. They may smile as they bring complaints to your attention, at the same time appear angry and insist that whatever is the source of their complaint is someone's responsibility, and that it can be remedied—by you. At the same time they are complaining, they are also expressing a measure of confidence because they are certain that a remedy for their dissatisfaction will be found; that they can depend on you if you pay attention to their complaint. They may be angry, but they are not mean.

Work through the angry, upset reproach as a complaint, and not as anger. By all means, grant their right to complain. Take their complaints and criticism seriously. All too often, their complaints have some merit. In that case, thank the complainer for bringing the matter to your attention. This is not a time to say, "Nevermind, it's not important." Or try to disregard or ignore the complaint, which enflames the angry complainer more.

Waiting is especially prone to provoke angry complaints. In the case of a long wait, validate the person's inconvenience and delay, and apologize. Tell them that you are keeping tabs on progress, and follow-up, such as "We are working on getting you in, it will be another 10 minutes, we haven't forgotten you." Without the follow-up, the patient will think they have been side-tracked and anger rises. An unexplained delay soon becomes intolerable, but an explained delay seldom reaches a crisis point.

One's tendency is to reciprocate angry behavior with angry behavior, but do not reciprocate in this way. Stay in control. Stay calm. Don't appear frightened. If the patient sees that they are causing 'squirming' or reaction in the medical staff, anger tends to escalate, and anger may escalate into violence.

Whatever stance you take, it must be non-threatening. Arms at your sides. An open palm. Make eye-contact, but do not glare. Keep a distance of 4 to 6 feet. Stand at a 45 degree angle to them, facing somewhat away or tangentially to the complainer rather than facing them directly; it is difficult to be angry with someone not standing directly facing you. If seated, do not have a table or any other furniture between you and the complainer. An interspersed table or bed or any other sizeable object gives the angry complainer a position of safety from which to show anger without fear of reprisal. Sitting or standing to the side of the table or bed brings you into closer proximity with the angry complainer which defuses some of their anger and threat.

As people grow increasingly angry, they become less rational and more prone to physical action. Be aware of body-language: flushed face, body stiffening, gritting teeth, glaring, and moving offensively close. Blood goes from the brain to large muscles, they are pumped, and they are ready for combat. If this point of escalation is reached, cause a hesitation, ask a question of the angry complainer. Ask exactly what they think they need so that you can assist them. The intent is to interrupt the angry spiraling of behavior and to get the individual to think logically, and for *them* to say what they think needs to be done. The volatile person tries to get you upset and angry, and to back down. When both parties are aroused into anger and confrontation permits no hope of a favorable solution to an angry complaint.

Staying calm, speaking softly, and affirming your intent to assist helps to keep the situation under control. Say, "I must understand the situation first so that I can help." The angry individual sees that further anger is not going to gain them anything. By enlisting the angry individual's response, the question draws them into finding a solution. The angry person feels powerless, so by appealing to their logical, verbal strength, their anger tends to dissipate.

Granting the person's position and acknowledging that they are upset and experiencing personal pain and frustration, also tends to dissipate anger. Logical statements or explanations or appealing to the inexplicable workings of God do not work. Understanding is what the angry person seeks, not explanation.

Dr. Dan Paulk recommends that when an individual "crosses the line between appropriate demands and personally insulting behavior," it's time for escape, which is especially true if you are alone in a room with an angry individual. Call for an interruption, "Time out. You are doing some things that are personally insulting to me and not appropriate." If possible, give the person a chance to save face by withdrawing their offensive statements. And if this fails, tell them you will have to leave or call the security guard. Edge toward the door. If a security button is available, use it. Angry people go from verbal to physical abuse if they perceive they are gaining the upper hand.[3]

An angry, upset complainer disturbs the entire Unit, disrupts care, and consumes extraordinary time and energy of the staff. Recognition and intervention as early as possible saves enormous trials and grief that may come later. Once the angry complaint is resolved, the angry complainer tells everyone. The angry, upset complainer often becomes an advocate for the hospital service just as emphatic and enthusiastic as their complaining once their complaint has been resolved, once they are able to trust. They may even help in resolving other patients or family's complaints or misunderstandings.

D. THE HELP-REJECTING COMPLAINER

The distrustful nature of the Help-Rejecting Complainer (HRC), or 'bear-trapper', is not apparent at first, but soon becomes so. The HRC complains about a problem to the helper, often with overtones of pathos, ill-treatment, or bad luck, enlisting feelings of a sense of obligation in the helper and a need to try to solve the complainer's problem. The complainer spins his or her web expertly. The helper makes a suggestion and an offer of assistance, which the complainer rejects, but the complainer reiterates his or her need for help, further entrapping the helper. The helper again offers a solution or aid, which the complainer again rejects with a feeling of despair and fading hope, which causes discomfort in the helper spurring the helper to redouble efforts.

Further offers of aid to resolve the complainer's complaint are systematically, serially rebuffed by the HRC saying each has been tried in the past and failed, often to ill effect, or an objection to the proposed solution. A contest develops

---

[3] Dan Paulk. "How to handle employee an patient violence." *Medical Office Manager* 6-8 (March) 1999.

between the helper and the help-rejecting complainer in that the helper feels challenged, then defeated and undermined by the complainer. The complainer further agitates the helper by saying that surely his sincere trust in the helper will be fulfilled, that he or she has every confidence and trust in the helper to come through as a last resort. The match goes on until the helper exhausts all possible options to aid the complainer, which the complainer finds satisfying by rejecting them all. The helper becomes frustrated, confused, and angry with the complainer or, at times, angry with himself or herself.

A clue to the help rejecting complainer is the blandness by which offers of advice are rejected, and the persistence of the complaint, which maintains the hold or grip the complainer claims on a helper. The complainer goes from helper to helper expressing disappointment that all others failed, but expresses hope and confidence that the new helper will succeed where all others have failed. The HRC may be bland or overtly hostile and aggressive, which puts additional stress on therapeutic attempts of the helper, which soon becomes hopeless to the helper. Trust is thoroughly destroyed, even though the HRC expressed the greatest trust and confidence at the outset.

Once the HRC has exhausted the helper's every offer of help, the helper often reacts with frustration and anger, and labels the complainer a 'nut', 'crock', 'neurotic', or other pejorative characterization that prejudices others in their interactions with the complainer.

If the HRC is overbearing and angry, the helper feels threatened and endangered, as well as frustrated and angry. The complainer departs with wishful feelings of disappointed hope that surely someone else can solve, which the helper finds injurious to his or her professional self-esteem. Once the complainer is gone, the helper vents anger and frustration towards the HRC, and sometimes the helper has a feeling of wanting revenge on the HRC who has defeated the helper. And in the case of a hostile, aggressive HRC, the helper may want to lash out verbally or physically.

The HRC must have control of the situation, and does so by placing obstacles before the helper. In this way, the HRC frees himself from the obligation to take charge of his own destiny because no matter what happens, someone else is at fault. The HRC may be able to manipulate their circumstances in such a way that the activities of an entire medical unit or family circle devote their lives to placating the pathetic or demanding needs of the HRC, but always failing. Redoubled efforts or a feeling of indebtedness follows failure to satisfy the HRC.

After a reasonable number of offers to help or therapeutic plans have been scuttled by the HRC, the helper must come to the realization that he or she is dealing with a HRC who is determined not to be satisfied in that all offers to help are rejected. Often a 'visceral' reaction precedes this awareness in that the helper feels frustrated and a growing feeling of exasperation, anger and annoyance.

Once the 'diagnosis' has been made, the helper stands back in a non-threatening posture and confronts the HRC by saying, "You have an objection to every possible solution" and waits, remains *silent*. The helper may feel great unease since he or she may feel that their responsibility to be helpful has failed. In addition, the helper may feel overwhelmingly threatened in the case of the aggressive and overbearing HRC.

The helper has now taken charge, and the HRC must respond. The HRC now knows intuitively that the tables have been turned. Rarely does the HRC react with anything except surprise, or an acknowledgement that the statement is correct. The statement will not be challenged. Often, the HRC deftly changes the subject, or quietly departs, never to be seen again. Although it takes considerable courage to confront the HRC the first time, subsequent confrontations are surprisingly easy and productive.

The first time I confronted a HRC, a hearty, athletic young man, I had one foot towards the door. The HRC looked at me blankly for an instant, and began to laugh. He said, "That's right, I do have an objection to everything."

The most important outcome is saving the helper from the HRC's trap, through an awareness that the unhappiness of the HRC is not of the helper's doing, nor can the helper expect to gratify the HRC's needs to be in control. Although trust was the basis for the encounter, the HRC cannot trust and had no intention of establishing trust with any helper but to undermine efforts by all helpers while presenting impossible demands for assistance.

The shift in power may be subtle, and occasionally quite dramatic, but rarely leads to verbal confrontation or physical abuse. The HRC is somewhat different from the ordinary complainer, in that the HRC complaints may be defused, but do not satisfy the HRC need for control. Usually, the HRC disappears, somewhat disheartened, sometimes amused, with no expression of gratitude, but knows that he or she has been bested. Seldom do HRCs become loyal to a physician or establish rapport with a helper, nor do they remain in a therapeutic situation or try to regain control once they have lost their advantage. They move on, many more unsuspecting helpers to conquer.

If intervention is not followed, the HRC remains in control. Frustration, anger, striking out, and other dysphoric behavior may occur in the helpers and staff. Staff or therapists may quit or try to ignore the HRC. A malignant form of HRC may report the staff or helper to a supervisor or administration, sometimes entrapping the supervisor or administrator immensely compounding the problem. The entire team must be alerted to prevent a splitting of the staff which increases control by the HRC. To be effective, the team must remain united in dealing with an HRC. The HRC may be a patient, a family member, friend, or all of these put together. Survival is the goal: the establishment of trust a remote possibility.

The Passive Helper

An inversion of the Help-rejecting Complainer is the 'Passive Helper' who at the initial consultation, after presenting his complaints, says, "I'll do everything I can to help you, Doc."

Red flag! A prelude to undermining the doctor and all therapeutic plans. This individual appears *excessively* trusting, but not actually. If allowed to continue, the doctor becomes ensnared in a net of crossed purposes, excessive testing, consultations, and growing frustration and resentment.

The challenge must be met early and immediately by replying, "I'm fine. Whatever benefit that comes from my care is for you, not for me."

E. THE HABITUAL COMPLAINER

Complaining and assertively expressing personal feelings openly became a chic trend of behavior over the past several decades that carries over into medical care in verbally abrasive patients and families. Patients are more apt to complain when treated like numbers, if they feel "herded" and ignored, especially during periods of illness and experiencing a physical impairment. Medications may lower inhibitions and escalate behavior due to stimulation or confusion. Some medications, like adrenergic drugs, stimulate a false sense of power to the user and lowers inhibitions and control of anger and complaints.

Frustrations of dealing with insurance companies, and long waits at medical offices and hospitals bring patients to the office with "negative expectations." Particularly vulnerable are the lower level employees, aides, phlebotomists, receptionists, etc. who are most easily abused by abusive individuals. Under these conditions, critical, insulting, and abusive individuals can be expected, as seen frequently by emergency room personnel and pharmacists. When social inhibitions are lowered and drugs interact, complaints escalate and reasonable behavior retreats, especially in those who seem predisposed to a complaining nature.

Some habitual complaining behavior carries over from the everyday: An elderly patient was admitted to our Rehab Unit from a distant hospital. The patient's medical condition had deteriorated from the time he was evaluated for transfer to the time of admission to the Rehabilitation Unit, such that he was not able to participate in an acute rehabilitation program. The patient's middle-aged son stood across from me at the opposite side of the patient's bed. I patiently explained that he was not able to participate in the rehabilitation program and that the patient must be transferred to an acute ward. The son, strong and muscular appearing, flushed red-face, threateningly, glowered at me, and shouted "What are you going to do about it?"

He was holding on to the bedside-rail and shaking it menacingly. Again, I explained, but he would have none of it. Growing more angry and louder with each exclamation, he could not be salved by a logical explanation. I was at a loss as to what to do. Words were of no help. Further discussion, such as it was, was met with ever more severe criticism and threatening language. The room overflowed with anger and tension. Louder and more menacing with each passing moment, he shook the bed rails and looked like he was going to explode at any moment if his demand, whatever it was, was not immediately met.

In desperation, I motioned for him to step out in the hallway with me where we could talk, mostly to stall for time, hoping a lightning bolt would strike, or some brilliant idea would flash into my mind to end this horrible encounter. I had no notion of what I would say, or what further explanation to this fireball of hate might save the day, or save me from greater humiliation and trauma.

To my surprise, he refused to leave the room, and when I last saw him, he was holding onto the bed-rail with all his might. Wild horses couldn't drag him away. His glowing red face turned pale. Everyone else, the other family members, in the room sat motionless, petrified.

Now, as I stood in the hallway waiting for this noisy, abusive, and for all I knew, assaultive son to come out to do battle, I was more confused. What could I do to bring such an impossible situation to a conclusion?

As I made my way down the hallway to the elevator, a man sat, squatting against the wall like mechanics sit, said, "Hey, Doc. How's it goin?"

I restrained myself from a forthright answer since what was going through my mind was 'why does anyone want to do this thankless work?' How would my resume look to a headhunter? I gave him a stern but avoiding look, and stepped lively.

"Don't let it bother you, Doc. He's like this all the time."

I began to laugh, in a subdued way. Then I stopped and peered directly at him. He, too, was suppressing an inner merriment, that the patient's son was behaving as he behaves. The present situation did not cause his behavior, it merely brought it to the fore. Apparently, many previous occasions had prompted such outlandish language and threatening behavior in this individual: an example of verbal intimidation or 'normal' chronic, verbal bullying behavior. As Dickens observed, "the coward is lurking under the bully."[4] He wouldn't let go of his safety rail or abandon his security spot.

When I was in college, we had a student in the house where I lived who complained constantly. Nothing was so small or inconsequential that he could not complain about it. He began complaining on getting up in the morning, complained all day, and went to sleep at night with a complaint dying in his throat. And, no doubt, dreamt complaining dreams.

He wasn't so much angry or threatening, but his constant griping and complaining became wearisome. At dinner, before dinner, after dinner, during meetings, at parties, walking to classes, etc. There was no relief, no respite from his negative, complaining, verbal barrage.

One of our housemates coined the term 'gunching' for his complaining: to gunch, gunch, shall gunch, will have gunched, would have gunched, will have had gunched. He became known as 'The Guncher,' later abbreviated to 'Gunch.' To be so nicknamed, was the only thing he didn't complain—that is, gunch—about. It seemed natural to gunch. To gunch fit, he accepted it, and so did we.

For some, to complain is as natural as breathing. I suppose it is an acquired habit. Perhaps familial. Or cultural. Although to live on the Great Plains, to endure in times of difficulty and trial is valued and gunching is not: *ad astra per aspera*.[5] I doubt if it is part of the genome; the future may tell.

Thus, every complaint must be dealt with according to the nature of the guncher, sorry, complainer as well as the nature and validity of the complaint. As H.H. Munro noted, "Let un sink as swims."[6]

F. THE 'WHY' QUESTION

By means of the stock-in-trade of the Sybarites and other complaining individuals who employ incessant empty, wafty questions, the Sybarite attempts to take control of conversation and dominate the therapeutic situation. The need of the sick-Sybarite for control notwithstanding, the physician must gain and maintain control by patiently, but firmly, handling the probing queries of the

---

[4] Charles Dickens. "The Ruffian." In *The Uncommercial Traveler* Cited in George Goodin, "Competitive Conversations in the Dialogue of Dickens." *Dickens Quarterly* 18 (2001) 3-20.
[5] "To the stars through difficulties."
[6] H.H. Munro. "The Peace of Mowsle Barton." *The Complete Works of Saki*. Garden City, New York: Doubleday, 1976, p. 189.

distressed sick-Sybarite. But, beware of the 'why' question which the sick-Sybarite has mastered; it is not a question for information, rather 'why' is used to manipulate and exasperate the physician, for the 'why' question veils accusations and distrust, undermining communication and understanding.

Managing the "why" question followed by a negation, the *why-negation complex*, is sometimes the key to successful management of the Sybarite along with management of many other patients and families. The why-negation complex is either a statement or a complaint or a veiled accusation. Do not answer 'why' petitions directly, but ask them to explain what the sick-Sybarite means by the question. Focus on the *verb* of the question: "Why was I allowed to have butter on my tray?" is not a question, but a statement or complaint. Make sure the sick-Sybarite explains the meaning of the question or statement, demand an explanation of "allow."

I have found that if you give the Sybarite ample time to answer his or her questions *once*, then maintain a limit on repetitious questions, they can be held to some degree of reasonable behavior. When repetitious questions arise, courteously, but firmly say, "I have answered that question, what don't you understand?" The testing will continue, for the sick-Sybarite cannot be reassured. Being satisfied is not part of their nature.

The 'why question' followed by a negation becomes an entrapment for the unwary. Remember, 'why' is a statement or accusation: "why didn't," "why weren't," etc. cannot lead to a just or fair response or conclusion. No way. It is intended to destroy trust, destroy the questioned, to inflict permanent harm and devastation.

The 'why' question is a vicious crime against all humanity and civilization. What does a mother expect when she demands "why didn't you clean up your room?!" or "plate?!" or "why were you late?!" and innumerable variations? The child's response cannot be an explanation or reply, but results in frustration, anger, and resentfulness for what the child interprets as verbal punishment: all quite justified. No agreement will come from the 'why' questioning-parent or patient or family member.

Asking the 'why-questioner' to explain just what he or she means by 'why' may diffuse the situation, but all too likely it is the provocation of anger that has welled-up in the 'why-questioner.' Best to go around the *why-negation complex* and not confront it directly. By identifying the verb and focus your remarks and responses on it, the statement or complaint can be more reasonably dealt with.

It takes a great deal of presence of mind to analyze and find the verb when confronted by a testy, demanding, condescending Sybarite. Repeat the *why-negation complex* aloud while listening to your self. Then again if necessary.

Repeat it as often as needed until you have isolated the verb, and then you can respond: "Butter was not *allowed* but was placed on your tray inadvertently."

Regard the *why-negation complex* as a complaint. Make certain that you understand the complaint clearly. Ask for details, examples, if necessary. Stall. Let the absurd nature of the remark, *why-negation complex,* sink in. draw out any other complaints that may be harbored in the *why-negation complex.* If no proper response is forthcoming, say that you don't understand what they mean, and that you must understand before the complaint can be satisfied. Anger, passive hostility at a fever pitch rides in the *why-negation complex.* Refuse to try to understand, and if necessary, walk away shaking your head in bewilderment rather than be entrapped in the *why-negation complex* which can not be brought to a reasonable conclusion until it is clarified.

The 'why questioner' is the Vice President of Criticism who is a disciple of, and make their ablutions to, the Greek god Momus (Hesiod and Aesop), the god of censure and ridicule, fault-finder, hypercritical: the god of Carping Criticism. No doubt the why-questioner was treated in this manner at a formative period and it stuck.

Make every attempt to change "why" question, to 'What is going on?' 'Why' turns us off, provokes bitterness.

A few other code-words that compromise trust to be aware of:

"Trying" a code for "not." Which avoids responsibility and accountability.

"Don't have enough time." Which means poor priorities. Shift priorities to take advantage of time. Playing the 'Time-Victim Card' of failure makes only a feeble attempt at adapting without taking responsibility.

"But" destroys what's in front of it. Use "and" or new sentence.

All of this is meant to gain equal footing with the 'why-questioner' because they are hell-bent on distrust, maintaining control when the situation requires that they partially relinquish control in order to be able to receive communication and information that they may not want to hear. Ethicists may balk at an imposition on a person's decision-making or individual liberties. Nevertheless, the circumstances of the patient's plight cannot be remedied by the Sybarite's or the 'why-questioner's' normal *modus vivendi* of divisiveness, self-interest, and distrust.

Like the two year-old child who has mastered the word "why," repeated endlessly, questioning results to the bewilderment and frustration of parents and elders who try to end the why-questions with explanations. Unless limits are observed, the child masters the adult. And the 'why-negation question' carries the day to everyone's discredit.

Chapter 3

CONFRONTATION

A. STREET FIGHT

After a few years in medical practice, I noticed that a few patients came to the office to argue and to verbally fight. They were not interested in my medical opinion or treatment so much as to have a face-off with someone. Seldom did they get recommended tests or take prescribed medicines. Some of these patients were angry, and some were not. The common denominator of distrust was spoken with an air of disdain and sometimes with an amused satisfaction measured to destroy earnest attempts to answer questions or "get to the bottom of things."

I eventually learned that argument, being their style of coping or *modus vivendi*, was their manner of daily interactions with everyone about them. Deflating egos is their specialty, especially those in any sort of position of authority or mastery. My attempts to change the tenor of our consultations uniformly met with failure and frustration. Annoyance soon followed, and I found myself hoping they wouldn't return since the encounters appeared to be hopelessly unsatisfactory. But alas, they returned with much the same style and demeanor. They seemed to revel in my discomfort and unease, when I thought I should at least be on even ground with them, since I am not a paternalistic or necessarily controlling physician.

All civil thoughts and practices of ordinary courtesy exhausted, I decided to verbally 'spar' with a few of these contestants. I egged them on ever so gently. Initially, I was quite wary and a little apprehensive about their response. Whether to have one foot towards the exit, or a policeman outside my door, or my hand on an alarm buzzer, just in case, crossed my mind. Nevertheless, it seemed I had nothing to lose by doing so, and little to gain by not challenging and sparing with them.

Much to my amazement, nothing much happened except the patients seemed to relax a bit and sit back a little in their chairs, and I sensed a bit of relief. I, too, sensed relief in myself. The argumentative style was not so much a threat as a way of communicating, communicating something, I was never certain exactly what, but the pressure of anger or *sub rosa* hostility was reduced. When faced with someone who is not willing to spar or 'dispute,' these individuals are unable to show them respect or establish trust. Only in the 'crucible of fire' can they find what they respect and trust.

According to Nobelist Peter Medawar, in the absence of absolute truth, the closest one can get to the truth is the ability of an idea, hypothesis or institution to withstand criticism, examination and attack. One doesn't know who one is until faced with adversity and criticism or attack, which these individuals are pleased to provide, *gratis*. Rather than feeling cornered or in a defensive position in coping with these skirmishes, which in fact are only words, they afford a chance for a sense of mastery to be achieved. At Cambridge University, England, students during examinations are called 'wranglers' for the style of argument used in disputations in examinations. Academic theses are 'defended' by candidates for doctorate degrees from intense scrutiny or challenge by the academy; only then can the validity of a thesis be trusted and held in esteem.

I concluded that the practice of medicine is much like a street-fight, or at least a disputation not necessarily on my terms. The rules are the same, only the pace is slower, although the stakes are about equally high. Once I recognized this facet of human nature, I began to recognize it in many other circumstances. That only by testing under-fire can some patients be satisfied. The doctor must verbally "take-up arms" in these circumstances so that the requirement of a common language can be achieved, and then most of the time communication actually improves. Don't expect a change in behavior, but the vehemence of the contest is defused. One must choose carefully and be willing to learn and think on your feet or use your feet for escape, but the rewards are peace of mind and a sense of security.

No longer did I feel defeated or frustrated by these people, but I secured a sense of mastery–principally of myself, and that I was not mastered by these naturally contentious people. They are only seeking truth and an ability to place trust in the physician. Once their manner or language was understood, rapport was much more acceptable. With this change in the human interaction of doctor and patient I felt much more satisfied with being a physician in situations that can easily cause frustration and burn-out. In addition, I think I became a better doctor at the same time. Many of these patients became and are still friends as well as patients. The challenge never stops, but the affect and mutual appreciation enhanced. Trust was built on a common language.

B. INTIMIDATION

Intimidation: in other words, bullying. The bully or intimidator retains the behavior of a child of about 6 years old. Trust in someone else is not readily one of their abilities, but to trust no one, using forceful ways overcomes resistance. Often bullying without provocation, when in situations encountering doctors and other healthcare professionals, old ways come forth.

Bullying plays a prominent role in daily human affairs. Certainly seen in traffic, at the store, in the streets, banks, and schools. "If you don't do such and such, you are going to regret it!" A great deal of sports is intimidation. The Sumitomo wrestler stalking about the center ring, scowling at opponents, tossing salt into the ring intends to intimidate his opponent. The baseball pitcher glowering down from atop the pitcher's mound, threatens a high-inside pitch to intimidate the batter. 'Trash talk' of basketball players serves to disturb a good player off the rhythm of his or her game. In quiet games like billiards, some players resort to bullying, intimidation to 'shark' opponents by a number of subtle methods.

Intimidators attack whoever is in front of them, and go from one to another seeking the weakest person to intimidate. Intimidators resort to bullying in most any and every situation, consistent in style, even though it might be as counterproductive for an adult as it was when a child.

The intimidator does not trust, but destroys trust. When placed in a situation requiring his or her trust, the intimidator reacts accordingly, but different from what we might expect or wish for. Once they see that the tactic of intimidation is not working, the intimidator may make an 180 degree turn-around into a fawning servility for a time.

Patients who have serious, lengthy illnesses may be accompanied by their mate or companion who is the intimidator. They go from ward to ward, unit to unit, with the same demeanor of trying to intimidate whoever is next, whether doctor, nurse, or therapist.

Doctors are great intimidators, as has been pointed out. Doctors teach by intimidation, learn by intimidation, and practice by intimidation.[1] Perhaps because

---

[1] Steven B. Enright. "How to sell doctors almost anything." *Medical Economics* Dec. 21 (1992) 75-80.

much of medical practice is overshadowed by uncertainty, an air of overbearing authority supplants certainty. So, the scene is set for confrontation if one is not careful and aware of the nature of the intimidators.

William Hazlitt remarks, "Opposed to these are the swaggering bullies–the licensed wits–the free-thinkers–the loud talkers, who, in the jockey phrase, have *lost their mouths*, and cannot be reined in by any regard to decency or common-sense."[2]

Charles Dickens' many comments about encounters with intimidating, disagreeable people are important in dealing with bullies and intimidators. About Jonas Chuzzlewit, Dickens says,

> "conscious that there was nothing in his person, conduct, character, or accomplishments, to command respect, he was greedy of power, and was in his heart, as much a tyrant as any laurelled conqueror on record."

Supporting this theme are Dicken's stable of bullies: Ralph Nickleby, Dombey, Jaggers, and dozens of others. Dickens says that Bumble "had a decided propensity for bullying: derived no inconsiderable pleasure from the exercise of petty cruelty; and, consequently, was (it is needless to say) a coward."[3]

Recognizing the bully is not always eaasy. Some are obvious, large, loud, and loutish. Others are frail-appearing, wring their claw-like hands, wear thick glasses, and bound forth from all genders, codes and creeds. Some intimidators hire their work done for them by assistants or retain attorneys who behave according to their contract or professional responsibility of intimidation.

When confronted by an intimidator, one must use tact and self-assurance which tends to disarm the bully. They are prepared for a frontal assault on the weakest link. By showing that you are not weak and know what you are doing, the intimidator has been bested for the moment. One wants to react in kind, which our natural juices call up, but maintain control of yourself and the situation. It is only talk and will likely remain talk unless the intimidator is cornered. Always allow the intimidator an out, an escape. In rare instances, when cornered and forced, the intimidator may strike out in the most extreme and inept way. Like the Angry Complainer, the Intimidators are behaving as they characteristically behave.

Intimidators, or confrontationalists, recognize each other as if they wear an invisible, red "C" around their necks, visible only to other confrontationalists.

---

[2] Hazlitt, William. *Selected Essays of William Hazlitt*. Editor Geoffrey Keynes. London: Nonesuch. New York: Random House, 1946. p. 328.
[3] Charles Dickens. *Oliver Twist* (1838). cited in George Goodin, "Competitive Conversations in the Dialogue of Dickens." *Dickens Quarterly* 18 (2001) 3-20.

Flushed, clammy, arched neck and shoulders, jaws clenched, they stand toe-to-toe with their kind and jaw in a most threatening and comical way. Rarely does anything more come of it, but it seems to clear the air for them for a little while. Confrontations of this sort are inappropriate in medical encounters and best defused as soon as possible, although confrontations with intimidators are mostly puffing and wheezing. Once the intimidator or confrontationalist sees that their tactic is not going to be matched with similar puffing and wheezing, they settle to whatever level is established by the therapy team.

Intimidators do not change, but remain on the scene looking for any possible abasement of their limited ability to trust. Do not expect apologies for outrageous behavior. Do not expect gratitude. A draw is the best you can expect, and in fact, successfully dealing with an intimidator can be very gratifying, for it means that the entire therapeutic or medical unit is functioning as it should. The intimidator leaves a legacy of black humor behind; if resentment follows, staff training and coaching in dealing with these challenging situations is necessary.

C. THE HATEFUL PATIENT

"But ye *are* forgers of lies, ye *are* all physicians of no value." *Job* xiii: 4.

Certain difficult patients go several standard deviations outside the norm, distrustful patients in the extreme, the hateful patient. Dr. James E. Groves provides useful guidance in dealing with these hateful, friendless souls.

The hateful patient assumes a searing, destructive, assaultive demeanor to physicians and therapy staff. Negative feelings or aversion by doctors and medical staff inevitably follow, and sometimes the patient receives unfavorable labels: "exasperating," "demanding," which may lead to dificult confrontations. The hateful patient often provokes feelings of "helplessness of the helpers," self-incrimination in the doctors and staff, and avoidance. Nevertheless, they cannot be wished away.

That the hateful patient exists must be acknowledged, yet doctors and staff have little to go on in dealing with them. The hateful patient must be recognized and dealt with in as professional manner as possible under the circumstances. No attempt to 'analyze' the hateful patient is attempted here, but like other difficult, distrustful situations, behavior alone is considered.

Recognizing the nature of the hateful patient may be obscured by the intensity of negative feelings within the doctors, nurses and therapy staff. Negative feelings in the helpers has been likened to the occasional hateful feelings of a mother toward her fussy, demanding infant: "Down will come baby / Cradle and all." Counter-hateful feelings under these circumstances are inevitable, and doctor and staff must be shielded from feelings of failure or guilt provoked by these immensely trying encounters.

Equally important is understanding that the hateful patient acts hatefully in other aspects of his or her life, and behaves in kind when in a medical circumstance. Survival of the medical team takes on importance as well as the medical needs of a hateful patient.

"Entitled demanders" describe the hateful patient where neediness is marked by intimidation, devaluation and guilt-production in medical personnel. They brook no compromise toward physicians or nurses, nor do they show empathy for anyone else. The hateful patient exhibits a repulsive sense of an innate deservedness, as if they were far superior to the physician and members of the therapy team, which shields them from awareness that physicians seem to the hateful patient as having the power over life and death.

Their hostility arises from terror of abandonment resorted to by the hateful patient to preserve integrity of the self in a world that seems hostile and threatening, and during an illness that seems terrifying. They tend to reject, when they demand what they feel they deserve, and require a "tireless repetition of the theme of acceptance that the patient deserves first-rate medical care."

The hateful patient is unaware of his or her dependency underlying their attacks, they lay hold on the physician by threatening punishment, threatening litigation or other entrapping behavior. Their feeling of "magical entitlement" to everything wanted becomes depressing, and often enraging to the physician and staff whose knowledge and competency is challenged, and they may feel shamed and threatened as if the hateful patient's demeaning, insistent demands were real. Entitlement may serve the hateful patient in the same way that "faith and hope serve in better adjusted ones," a quasi-religion that must not be blasphemed.[4]

Dr. Groves suggests physicians and therapists support the entitled demander by redirecting them into the therapeutic program, but not capitulating to unreasonable demands or allowing them to bully or intimidate the staff. Avoid entanglement in frustrating logical, or illogical, debates with the hateful patient. The hateful patient is also socially inept and similar techniques may be useful.

Some needs are too deep in the hateful patient and expectations unrealistic: "Doctors, on the other hand, jeer at both tooth-pullers and herbalists, and are

---

[4] James E. Groves. "Taking care of the Hateful Patient." *New England Journal of Medicine.* 298 (1978) 883-887.

themselves treated as fools by their patients who expect to be kept alive with hearts or livers in a hopeless state..."[5].

Surviving a hateful patient is certainly not easy, nor are easy answers available. Physicians, therapists, nurses, and all other members of the therapy team must work together and support each other. In no other instance in medicine is a team approach more important. Solace to the stricken individuals of the therapy team is vital to the integrity of the staff, which must be supported in order to provide the care that the hateful patient requires but cannot himself or herself understand or appreciate. Gaining the trust of a hateful patient may not be possible, but putting boundaries on their behavior may permit the therapy team to act in the patient's behalf. Trust must be defined in a different way with the hateful patient; no expression of gratitude is expected, but a limited cooperation and completion of the therapy program is itself the reward for their care.

Strangely, hateful as they may be, an illogical occurrence of appreciation from the hateful patient may be seen long after their discharge from the hospital by their seeking care once again for themselves or people that they refer for care. They may not be able to express gratitude or trust, but their criticizing other professionals in your presence serves as a covert compliment and expression of gratitude.

Elster says, "As Aristotle noted [*Politics* 1312^b 19-34] the angry man is irrational whereas the man animated by hatred is not, although the emotion may be grounded in an irrational belief."[6]

D. VIRULENT VISITORS. THE SCHMOO ENIGMA

While visits by comforting relatives and friends may be welcome and beneficial to patients in the hospital or ill at home, occasionally, visitors are virulent and destructive to patient care. Some visitors may be well-meaning but misguided when they bring a mariache band to entertain a patient who is nauseated and vomiting; others expect to be entertained by the patient who is in pain, fatigued or under the effects of pain-relieving medicines. Visitors can be exhausting to patients as well as tiresome if they over-stay their welcome. Playing the television or their portable radio loudly takes away from patients' rest and sleep.

---

[5] Giuseppe Di Lampedusa. *The Leopard*. Translated by Archibald Colquhoun. Giangiacomo Feltrinelli Editore, 1958. New York: Pantheon, 1960, p. 229.
[6] Elster, Jon. "Emotions and Economic Theory." *Journal of Economic Literature* 36 (1998) 47-74.

Patients in the hospital are especially vulnerable and unable to control unwelcome visitors setting up the possibility of abuse and victimization. Some visitors take the opportunity to square old grievances while they have the advantage. At times, visitors arrive at wrong times, such as after a diagnostic procedure or after surgery when the visitor expects light, social conversation. Large families or clubs or coworker, all arriving at the same time, crowd into the patient's room to have a jolly time while ignoring needs of the patient. Visitors may wish to be humorous and make the patient laugh "to cheer them up" when the patient most wants to be left alone.[7]

Visitors are adept at undermining trust in many ways. Some visitors, being amateur doctors, question the patient's diagnosis and treatment. Others frighten patients by suggesting horrible illnesses and tragic outcomes as if the patient should be interested in their thoughtless and cruel remarks. A doleful recitation of the visitor's own troubles and trials to the invalid-patient reverses the direction of caring from patient to the visitor when the patient is most in need of comforting themselves; the patient feels an obligation to be comforting to the visitor.

Derogatory remarks by visitors about the hospital or its staff interferes with the patient's morale and sense of quiet and undermines confidence and trust in the hospital or the doctors. Suggesting a less than optimal outcome by "someone I know" undermines hours of sleep and rest needed for recuperation. Uncertainty, fear and foreboding the evening before surgery wreak havoc on the confidence and trust of a patient at a most defenseless time.

Hospital visiting policies change from time to time, and doctors are well advised to keep abreast of changes. A doctor may make his or her own rules for a particular patient by ordering a sign on the patient's door of no visitors, so the nurses can monitor who visits and allow those who are approved to visit by the patient. Limiting visitors may be critical for some patients.

The doctor may assist patients by asking about visitors and whether visitors are welcomed and comforting. Advising patients not to discuss their medical status with visitors and only in vague generalities aids in preserving the patient's peace of mind. Occasionally, if a visitor is especially intrusive, the patient is encouraged to ask the visitor to change the subject or to leave for the time being. Often well-meaning visitors don't realize they are out of place or their conversation is unpleasant and unwelcome, and appreciate being reminded not to over-tax the patient.

---

[7] Walter E. O'Donnell. "When problem visitors rile your hospital patient." *Medical Economics* April 14, 1997, 220-222.

Distrustful visitors or relatives who are disruptive to the workings of a hospital unit may regard medical personnel like Al Capp's Schmoos in *Lil' Abner*: colorless, roundish, globular, perpetually smiling, non-resisting, oafish, ghost-like creatures that love to be kicked, the schmoo was the symbol of passivity, simplemindedness and masochism. Used largely in a political sense by its creator, the schmoo was not a very popular figure. The idea that people should be in the position of taking abuse as a matter of natural disposition may have provoked an uncomfortable humor, yet, the absurd perception of angry and distrustful people with the 'right' to be abusive to medical staff or other people was insightful by its author.

The schmoo-abusing individual is pictured as being moronic, over-bearing, and reprehensible. While the schmoo is the character depicted, it is the abusive, distrustful individual that is lampooned who acts in conformity with their previous or habitual behavior. They are on the lookout for those individuals who they consider as vulnerable as schmoos and treat them as they would expect schmoos want to be treated. Being aware of these predatory creatures and taking appropriate action prevents abusers from abusing the medical staff.

The truly malignant visitor who defies all avenues of reasonable attempts at control or limiting their abuse may cause turmoil and chaos on the entire hospital unit. Any semblance of trust is destroyed. Asking these intruders to leave may bring about ugly and occasionally violent responses. In private hospitals, the only people with a *right* to be in the hospital are those seeking medical treatment and those who work at the hospital. All others are either guests or, in a sense, trespassers. As a last resort, calling hospital security may be the only way to gain control and maintain patient and staff safety. If this fails, a call to the police may be necessary. Most important to remember, that nurses, doctors, and all other medical personnel are not there to be abused or to take abuse of any kind. Some visitors, like occasional patients, think that medical workers have no rights and are fair game for threats, verbal abuse, and violence. Visitors may arrive intoxicated or in the effects of street drugs making control and discipline more difficult.

A visitor refusing to cooperate with those in charge is an early warning sign of trouble. They spread rumors and gossip about the staff undermining trust of those around them, sometimes arguing with employees or with other visitors and patients. Extremes of behavior may occur if they are belligerent toward other people or other patients on the Unit, swear at staff members or other visitors, or make unacceptable sexual remarks.

If further escalation occurs, an emergency response must be available to the staff. If a visitor shows intense anger, destroys property, flashing weapons in threats to harm others, fighting or commission of violent acts, provokes extreme measures to control. A plan for such extraordinary behavior must include promptly calling security and, if necessary, the police.

The virulent visitor is principally interested in destroying trust and cooperation. It's their way of interacting with their world by provoking distrust, disorder, and turmoil. They are no longer visitors, but miscreants who threaten the staff and patients. Gentle, normal social interaction fails. Control is not easy. Rights of visitors give way to rights and protection of the safety of patients and staff.

E. MANAGED CARE MONSTER

Managed care brings out the worst in many already difficult, distrustful patients and creates a new level of distrust. The basic tenets of managed care are based on cynicism and distrust about both patients and medical care. Managed Care Monsters come in two general categories: the voluntary monsters who join a managed care plan of their own accord and the involuntary monsters who are placed in managed care by employers, government or other institutions.

Managed care by its very nature discourages people from seeking care that the managed care industry does not want to pay for, thus placement of deliberate barriers to the availability of medical care, and inapt barriers to receiving care. Patients and family, with some justification, feel angry that they are getting the run-around. By these tactics, suspicion and distrust are magnified.

The Managed Care Monster manages to avoid or circumvent their primary doctors, mistakenly called 'gatekeepers,' and go straight to the specialists, the opposite of the desires of the managed care industry. Often, this breach of managed care protocol is performed with great bombast, and noisy interaction. Distrust of the system of the managed care entity is at the focal point of the disturbance.

The young and healthy are especially attracted into managed care plans, yet they may feel that they are 'on loan' to the managed care industry's doctor. 'Here today, gone tomorrow,' all are transients: patients, doctors, hospitals, and managed care companies.

Those who are involuntarily enrolled in a 'vertically integrated' managed care plan may be particularly distrustful, as a young plumber called to our house said, "I've got $K-P-$, but I don't trust it."

Doctors pitted against each other, with loss of respect between doctor and doctor, distrust of old and new doctors, leads to fragmented care, and excessive administrative costs. Distrust of clerical personnel in managed care companies makes time consuming and frustrating demands for explanations and justifications of daily medical practice decisions. While many practices of the managed care industry are appalling, that so many were so easily duped–doctors, businesses, public, government, etc.–is astonishing, but hardly displaces or counters managed care's inherent level of distrust.

Capitation of those physicians who earn the least and bear the risks of managed care is both foolish and cynical. By the principle of "what-can-be-gotten-away-with," managed care claims managers appear to be responsible to no one. The managed care industry answers to businesses that purchase it, and businesses answer to stockholders. Whether care is provided or not has little influence on decisions of business. No wonder trust is subverted.

Gaining trust in a distrustful managed care 'environment' requires that the therapy staff care for patients as if managed care does not exist. What is reasonable and proper care does not vary according to method of reimbursement. Decisions to limit or deny care must be placed back on the managed care industry and those who purchase it; reasonable efforts on the part of the therapy team to intervene is mandatory, however, we can't fight every battle forever. Eventually, responsibility for decisions of the managed care industry's spokespersons must be dealt with in our society through representative government.

In the meantime, holding to basic principles and practices of medical care is the only way to develop a trustful relationship with a Managed Care Monster. The responsibility remains with the managed care industry.[8]

F. THE TELEPHONE TERRORIST

I was stupefied with fear; my hair stood on end and my voice stuck in my throat.

Vergil *Aeneid* II, 74

Like the confrontationalist-bully who attacks from a defensive position behind a table or counter, the Telephone Terrorist uses the expedience of the distance and intermediary of the telephone. To the terrorist, out to destroy rapport, confidence and trust, the telephone is convenient. Generous employment of the 'why' question, 'don't you realize,' and other verbal thrusts provoke unease and distrust. Rudely speaking-over replies of the doctor or nurse is standard practice

---

[8] R.D. Smith. *Rise and Fall of Managed Care: History of the Mass Medical Movement*. Hauppauge, NY: Nova Science Publishers, 2002.

so that no explanation can be completed. Gaining information or insight is not on the agenda of the Telephone Terrorist.

Telephone Terrorists provoke feelings of alarm, dismay, and consternation that may result in extreme fear in the presence or threat of danger or evil. Terror is an intense, overmastering fear that may be somewhat prolonged and refer to imagined or future danger. The Telephone Terrorist plays on invisibility and distance that intensifies the effect of their asocial, thoughtless charges against the recipients of their calls. Panic with uncontrolled unreasoning fear, often groundless, may be prolonged if the Telephone Terrorist is not identified and controlled. Terrorism in this context incites a state of fear and submission as a method of control. Telephone Terrorists seek to dominate or coerce by intimidation:

> I could a tale unfold whose lightest word
> Would harrow up thy soul, freeze thy young blood.
> Make thy two eyes, like stars, start from their spheres,
> Thy knotted and combined locks to part
> And each particular hair to stand on end,
> Like quills upon the fretful porpentine.
> *Hamlet*, Iv

The Telephone Terrorist is equally a bully, like Charles Dicken's definition of a coward. They seldom present serious threats, but cannot be disregarded.

Be polite, but firm. Try to interrupt and get their attention. "Sir. Sir. I can't get a word in edgewise." "How can I help you unless you are willing to listen?" If that is not possible, say, "When you are under control, perhaps we can talk again Till then, goodbye." And promptly hang up.

If you are not able to get their attention or break the stream of abuse, end the call as soon as possible. Do not listen to abusive language. If you are interrupted or they talk-over your reply, after the first instance, keep talking in a calm, even voice even though they are going on at a furious pace. The goal of the Telephone Terrorist is to cause chaos, testing, whether you can be trusted.

Allow a little time to pass. Later, when the fire has cooled, perhaps making contact, depending on the situation. Unless prepared, the Telephone Terrorist can upset or destroy you or your therapy staff. Gaining trust is impossible under these circumstances. As onerous as it may seem, scheduling a face-to-face meeting is much preferable to enduring the Telephone Terrorist at his or her worst.

G. Bad News

"Many illnesses are promoted from the third rate to the first-rate by the anxious mind."[9]

Anxiety precedes every diagnostic procedure and every therapeutic situation. The future, the unknown, brings phantasms of dread and foreboding. Even the most bold and courageous, the callous and cynical, develop a racing heart, cold and moist palms when facing something medically unknown. Their bluster and overbearing ways do not help them now. Doctors and nurses, too, perhaps more so, fret about the outcome of test results even though they may have every reason to feel at ease. Medical personnel know more things to worry about. It's facing the future, the ultimately unknown that holds all sorts of shadows and dark alleys. No matter their previous experience or other medical illnesses and treatments, their ability to trust is under maximum dissection.

Nothing creates more distrust than the time needed in the evaluation and decisions of a complex case. All sorts of heeby-jeebys come out of the woodwork to haunt patient, family, relative, and friends. The only apt response by the physician is "time will tell," which may inflame further passions of doubt and distrust.

"There is something worse than knowing the worst. It is not knowing – one has to know. There are worse things than bad news."[10]

Good news passes quickly, that is, when the tests are negative and reassuring. But when the examinations and tests lead to serious consequences, the bearer of the news may be challenged and distrusted. It's the agonizing period in between that is most troublesome. Sometimes, a number of telephone calls, or notes passed through the receptionist's window, or impromptu visits in the hallway of the office or hospital carry a sense of urgency and impatience. Sleepless nights, loss of appetite, pacing about, wringing of hands, and many other strange and unfamiliar habits and behavior come to the fore.

Working with doctors and therapy staff comes easily to most individuals, but the distrustful do not participate so easily. While criticizing any and all aspects of care, establishing trust is a major challenge. Pursuing a false hope is equally disastrous. Denial is a powerful human defense. Head in the sand, not facing the reality of a difficult course, leads towards a greater disaster, and distrust.

---

[9] Eric Partridge. *New York Times* 2 June 79.
[10] Walker Percy. *Lancelot*. New York: Farrar, Straus, Giroux, 1977, p. 131.

Strange to say, reassurance that anything can be faced once known may be a comfort for the moment, but only finally knowing settles the anxiety, alleviates distrust. Not knowing is the worst.

Chapter 4

BIG SHOT

A. RETURN OF THE SYBARITE: THE NEGLECTED PARENT CONSTELLATION

The out-of-town Sybarite who arrives from the far side of the country to visit a sick relative may be especially difficult. Sickness in another is especially onerous to the out-of-town Sybarite because his or her social or professional schedule has been interrupted by the workings of events far away and due to "something that should never have happened." The illness of a neglected relative may be the only occasion for a genuine or recent contact between the Sybarite and his or her ailing family member, sometimes a number of years. Recognizing the phenomenon seems easy, but in practice they may cause so much turmoil that the staff becomes entangled in their demands, anger, and airy repetitious why-questions.

When a sick-Sybarite's parent becomes ill, the Sybarite flies in from the Great City and demands to know why this and why that, intent on making an impressive show of caring and concern in the only manner they know. Demeaning and demanding to the medical and nursing staff, they create great smoke and flurry and commotion while remaining aloof to perils of the patient. Much anger and impatience is expressed making a thin over-lay of guilt as well as a poorly covered-up expression of fear.

In order to cope with the out-of-town Sybarite, recognition is essential. They obtrude into the hospital or office with an abundance of commotion and fury and noise. Demanding a meeting with everyone in authority, hypercritical is their *modus vivendi*. The Quality Assurance Office tops their list of places to visit where they are regular visitors. If unaware, the administration may be caught in their demonstrations of "appalling concerns," who escorts them to the Rehabilitation Unit for a conference with the staff who they expect to bring all efforts to bear on the Sybarite's parent, and never mind the medical needs of other patients.

As a friend who worked for a major utility company said of similar circumstances, "Kill them with kindness. Let them run about for a time, then tell them you will look into it." Patience is essential and always remain respectful toward the out-of-towners, even though the staff is well aware that their exaggerated demonstration of caring is largely false and a put-on. Sometimes their complaining manner is disguised in sweetly phrased why-questions, but mask a poorly disguised hate. By recognizing that the why-questions are not appeals for information, but they are complaints, treat their questions as complaints.

The angry Sybarite-son or daughter claiming to look out for the welfare of an aged parent, for instance, cares little that the patient may have little chance of recovery, otherwise the angry Sybarite off-spring wouldn't be in town. Even though the patient, aka loved-one, may be "circling-the-drain," the Sybarite wants whatever the trouble might be 'fixed' and wants it fixed right now. That is, why hasn't this been done before? and why hasn't that been done? and why does in take so long? These are not questions, but statements of frustration and distrust. And if it can't be 'fixed,' then "get it over with."

Dealing with the Sybarite under these circumstances requires that their uncomfortable and distressed position be acknowledged and that the staff will work with them as best as possible in a non-judgmental manner. The temptation to reply in kind or to shame or provoke guilt on the Sybarite is never permitted; if allowed, would be immensely counter-productive.

If a child is ill, the Sybarite demonstrates their worst nature: angry and worried that the child may become a burden or interfere with the Sybarite's own, self-indulgent pursuits. A show of caring and affection may be mistakenly expressed in anger or aloofness towards the staff, and even the most basic social graces are ignored, placing great strain on the sense of humanity of the medical staff who are largely middle class with values that are very different from those of the Sybarite from afar. Similarly, the Sybarite's mate/spouse remains true to form, blandly interested in showing an acceptable degree of involvement, but alertly seeks to know whether or not the affliction of their otherwise beloved is contagious, i.e., a threat to their own health and well-being: always on the lookout for Number One.

The out-of-town Sybarite can be an interesting challenge. Taking the distressed Sybarite into your confidence may accomplish wonders. Achieving an understanding of the complexities of medical illnesses by the out-of-town

Sybarite and the necessary medical decisions about their relative is not always possible, but compassion may be met with an emotional leveling. The staff may become split as to how to cope with the out-of-town Sybarite, thus having an advance plan in place beforehand may head off a great deal of trouble and distress in the medical staff. Once rapport is achieved and the Sybarite is able to trust the new, unfamiliar physicians and staff, this brand of Sybarite may actually soften a bit and become more reasonable

In the event of the recovery or death of the patient, the true Sybarite from out of town disappears like a flash of lightning. And gratitude?

B. BIG SHOT FROM OUT OF TOWN

The Big Shot from Out of Town (BSFOT) is a subtle nuance on the Neglected Parent Constellation. The angry Sybarite called to town by the illness of a relative is mostly pretense; the blustering Big Shot has credentials. President of a corporation, head of a firm, CEO of a Fortune 500 Company, they know how to get things done and how to make people miserable. To quote one, "I've made a good living getting my own way."

The BSFOT comes in a variety of forms. Some are largely puffery, promoted beyond their abilities, they can be regarded as such. Nevertheless, they are just as difficult and often impossible to engage in their own care or their family member's care or they may be evasive to a fault and impossible to pin-down. They present something of a nuisance, but are generally tractable eventually, or they are so impossible and little can be accomplished with them. In extreme instances, as the head of a large clinic once said, the best that can be done is to get them out of town and back home as soon as possible.

In the event that the BSFOT is hospitalized, the entourage or circus follows. Some large medical centers cater to the BSFOTs with special suites and extra comfortable accommodations. The BSFOT can wheel and deal as soon as he or she awakens from anesthesia, though advised to wait. In this setting, the pace is generally slower in that the executive suites are not paid for by insurance companies, but underwritten by corporations or personal funds. Accustomed to pampering and luxury, the BSFOT is in no hurry to leave the comfort of their 'special' hospital rooms. The BSFOT may be the spouse of a BSFOT, where the demands are somewhat different. Every accommodation made to the BSFOT is intended to spare the working BSFOT inconvenience.

At the height of his or her powers, the BSFOT may be too involved in his or her business or profession by telephone, fax, or portable email to give the medical team time to work with them. Setting limits on outside activities can be a daunting undertaking, but establishing limits is essential to the successful management and medical treatment. Surrounded by subalterns and sycophants, the BSFOT looks at his or her own medical care as they would a number-painting: call out the numbers and someone else does it, who also is held accountable if anything goes amiss. Trust is not in the BSFOT's job description.

The BSFOT is remarkably like the intimidating bully, and, of all things, though over-socialized, is often socially inept. So, the same ideas suggested for the Confrontationists and Intimidators can be applied. Strangely, when treated in this way, they actually show respect to those who do not allow themselves to be intimidated or bullied. The meek and polite are their quarry, fair game, or cannon fodder, such that they may have everyone dancing on a string if they are permitted to run amok. Taking charge is not easy, but necessary and usually easier than expected aforehand. Granting that they are in charge of their corporation and you are in charge of matters medical establishes who is in charge of their medical care for the moment, the chain of command. Set the ground rules, and at the same time, be as flexible and reasonably possible without compromising patient care. A simple explanation at the outset to the BSFOT establishes the essential rules: that the BSFOT is in the hospital for medical treatment and that energy spent on outside activities detracts from efforts towards recovery, and hope for the best outcome. Often a spouse or relative, sometimes their secretaries, have more influence and common sense who may mediate for the therapy staff, nurses and doctors.

The press may be on site with their probing questions that must be directed to the Public Relations Department. Reporters may pry in unsuspecting ways, but the confidentiality of the BSFOT must be diligently observed. The flurry about the BSFOT captures attention that rightfully belongs to the rest of the patients on the Rehabilitation Unit or ward. Care must be taken to make sure that all other activities of patient care continue in the presence of the Out-of-Town Big Shot lest the rest of the patients and their families grow suspicious that not enough attention is being paid to them, which can be a genuine concern.

As the BSFOT recovers, a new phase of management begins, that of discharge plans. Never straight forward, numerous exceptions to reasonable arrangements surface. A meeting in Jamaica. A conference in Milan. A speech in London. A vacation in Tahiti. And "would you mind writing me a letter that I am able to go hunting in Labrador in the Fall?" Or a statement that they can get their health club membership extended gratis. Or their insurance or loan payments can be delayed for 'medical reasons.' The BSFOT is nothing if not cheap.

Nevertheless, eventually the BSFOT is discharged from the hospital. A sense of relief follows.

C. The Famous Person Constant

The Famous Person is somewhat different from the Big Shot from Out of Town. The Famous Person also considers himself or herself entitled to every possible service. Famous Persons have notice of the public. They may be familiar from their pictures in newspapers or appearance on television.

Entitled. That's the key word. Also aloof. Someone else will take care of it. They are also alone by the position they occupy, even though the Famous Person is surrounded by a circle of attendants and pursuviants. Famous Persons may be alienated and isolated by success and position or by inclination.

The subalterns of Famous Persons assume the privilege-of-station of the Famous Person, "chic bitchy," irritable, "carrying it with a high hand." They may be more difficult than the Famous Person himself or herself. The Famous Person's circle of sycophants demand 'extra service,' extra time, favors, and spare nothing. Famous Persons are quick to use doctors' and therapists' first names, though maintaining a safe distance for themselves. The unwary doctor, because of the affable and engaging sociability of a Famous Person may think that we are in the same league with the Famous Person, but when Famous Persons are in their natural habitat, we learn otherwise. Best to keep a safe and respectable distance.

Though a recipient of the affections of the world, the Famous Person is not necessarily happy or satisfied with their more or less exalted status. They may feel deficient or come to recognize that the public adulation is orchestrated or less than genuine. Sometimes the Famous Person becomes distrustful, since they are the focus of many charity appeals and they are the supporters of a cadre of attendants that don't always act in the Famous Person's best interest.

When in a medical setting, the Famous Person may be as engaging and hard working as anyone, or suspicious of everyone. Occasionally an attendant to the Famous Person demands credentials of the medical staff or visits to the kitchen, etc. No set pattern evolves for the Famous Person, except they are usually socially very affable and have a keen ear for anything that sounds suspicious. Being honest and forthright is always the best policy, and remains so with the Famous Person.

The trust of the Famous Person is a cautious wariness that never sleeps.

D. THE MACHIAVELLI PRINCIPLE: OR THE TOXIC HEALTHCARE PROFESSIONAL

Doctors, nurses, technicians, therapists, etc. Those who work with the sick and injured in the same capacity as those medical professional whom they criticize. Distrustful and angry, they throw their 'influence' around to impress the family or perhaps the staff of their importance, but succeed in creating a tragicomic scene with themselves as the one demeaned. Perhaps they are a variant of the 'toxic intern syndrome' with a pervasive cynicism, irritability mixed with anger, and irritation with staff support. Sometimes the Toxic Healthcare Professional takes on a passive-aggressive form striking back at doctors, nurses, and patients. In addition, 'scapegoating' is common in the Toxic Healthcare Professional, like the toxic intern, he or she vents anger against someone who has nothing to do with the case, or raises their voice in frustration in presence of the patient. Scapegoating may be carried on at home, and leveled against friends or family or complete strangers.[1]

The Toxic Healthcare Professional from far away observes no boundaries, often going into the nurses' station to use the telephone or the kitchen to help themselves to food or coffee or juice as if they were on the hospital staff or otherwise authorized. The Toxic Healthcare Professionals are intrusive, overbearing and rude to the extreme. Some use the fax machine without requesting permission, tie-up the telephone at the nurses station if permitted, and may even attempt to hack into the computer. On occasion, they park in restricted parking areas reserved for the hospital staff as if they were entitled. The Toxic Healthcare Professional is distrustful to the core.

Accusative, sullen and blame-laying, they may be loud and threatening, causing consternation in the staff and administration. The Toxic Healthcare Professional from away with a high nuisance-quotient consumes inordinate staff energy and concern. Blustery and loud, they expect to get their way, sometimes countermanding doctors' orders or interfering with care of the patient, and sometimes undermining care of other patients by their criticism of the care of all patients. The members of other patient's families and visitors become wary and frightened by the anti-social behavior of the Toxic Healthcare Professional.

The epitome of distrust, the Toxic Healthcare Professionals from away demand copies of everything. Questioning the most basic nursing activities or undoing what the staff has just done to make the patient more comfortable, the

---

[1] Kirsti A. Dyer. "Toxic Intern Syndrome." *Western Journal of Medicine* 160 (1994) 378-379.

Toxic Healthcare Professional interferes, obstructs, and denounces whatever is. Brusque and rude, they show no consideration to the patient or staff. They may attend family conferences with their yellow tablets and tape-recorders, unwillingly and at their leisure which, they assure us, is inconvenient.

One must wonder why such angry, disorderly, disagreeable people choose a career in medicine or an allied healthcare field in the first place? Wouldn't working in demolition be more to their natural aptitude? Maybe at wrestling matches or driving heavy construction equipment through forests, or crashing test cars?

Nevertheless, they are part of the circus of medicine. They flit and dive, scrape and scour, unaware of their futility and utter meaninglessness. A sense of relief and graveyard humor follows them when they are mercifully gone. Perhaps it's the Machiavelli phenomenon: that one does good works in medicine so that when the time is right, one has the right to be offensive and abusive, and to do evil with impunity. Where did they learn it? Is their behavior from example from another Toxic Healthcare Professional? Or is it indigenous to the particular individual?

Protecting the staff from the Toxic Healthcare Professional's demeaning, disgusting behavior becomes paramount. The Toxic Healthcare Professional delights in splitting the staff and creating confusion and chaos. On alert for anything to criticize, the Toxic Healthcare Professional from away seizes whatever opportunity is offered and manufactures whatever they can to disorganize the staff.

The staff must realize that the Toxic Healthcare Professional brought their anger and bitterness with them. The circumstances of the patient's illness or care play no role. The Toxic Healthcare Professional is several standard deviations off the norm. Way off the norm. You couldn't get them back to decent behavior with an arrest warrant, or a Sherman tank, or a nuclear weapon. Not a time to analyze.

Deal with their obnoxious behavior as obnoxious behavior, period. If they play the healthcare professional card, claiming they know what they are doing and the rest of the world is out of step, bring the socially inept healthcare professional's term of flight to an end as soon as possible. Reason and courtesy are of no use. They set the Toxic Healthcare Professional up for a loss.

Confronting their aberrant actions will not often bring the Toxic Healthcare Professional to rational behavior. Placing the responsibility for an unfavorable outcome due to their interference on them and not the responsibility of the hospital or staff usually helps. Setting limits is essential, and it is about all that can be done. Trust and gratitude from a Toxic Healthcare Professional will not be forthcoming. Maintain your own standards and principles, which will be severely challenged, but must be adhered to. In the end, the patient or other family members almost always acknowledge the behavior of the Toxic Healthcare Professional and the sick patient apologizes for the 'well' Toxic Healthcare Professional.

Chapter 5

PASSIVE DISTRUST

A. THE GUILT / SHAME DUALITY

Some authorities distinguish between cultures that rely heavily on fear of guilt and cultures that rely on fear of shame as sanctions for controlling behavior. The social roles of individuals can be brought under group control by means of enforcing conformity to an accepted standard of behavior based on these fears. The sanctions may be either internal by fear of the effects of guilt, or external by the fear of being ostracized from the social group by fear of shame.

A Catholic who is alone on an island, it has been said, rather than experience *internal* guilt would not eat meat on Friday. On the other hand, an American Indian alone on a lake, it has been said, would rather die than face *external* shame and ridicule if he should lose his oar and the means of propulsion of his canoe. All cultures have both internal and external sanctions, but cultures vary greatly in emphasis.[1]

Guilt acts as a proxy for long-term rewards that might otherwise fail to motivate the individual. That guilt is thought to be a cost to the individual, it is a tradeoff between moral emotions and self-interest. Human beings have an image of themselves as acting rationally: "Guilt, in this perspective, acts not as a cost but as a psychic force that induces the individual to rationalize his behavior. Beyond a certain point, when the arguments on the other side become too strong and the rationalization breaks down, a switch in behavior occurs."

In a guilt culture, an individual will obey internalized standards of morality without reference to outside forces. The person would respond to internal

---

[1] Robert C. Elliott. *The Power of Satire: Magic, Ritual, Art*. Princeton, New Jersey: Princeton University Press, 1960, pp. 66-69.

sanctions, following his conscience in order to avoid the negative effects of guilt. Violation would produce a kind of torment, which can be relieved only by confession or atonement.

Shame cultures rely on external sanctions to govern behavior: what other people will think or say, whether praise or blame, are over-riding considerations in actions of the individual. If wrongdoing becomes known, he will be criticized, shamed, rejected or ridiculed: ridicule in the most powerful form of public disapproval. Few horrors are dreaded more than to be publicly laughed at. Ridicule or fear of ridicule holds terrors sufficient to cause the most violent reactions against it, and at its extreme, includes suicide to rid the individual of the destructive force of ridicule. To be laughed at is more dreaded than suffering violence because it leads to ostracism and death by "emotional starvation."

Shame is intensely unpleasant; no one would ever seek it out. Yet a person might try to develop a disposition to feel shame or, more plausibly, to inculcate shame in others with the goal being the avoidance of shame feelings by avoiding occasions or abstaining from actions that might cause feelings of shame. An expression of contempt may induce shame if seen as spontaneous, but expressions of contempt cause anger if seen as intended to induce shame. People may take extreme actions when targeted by social ostracism. Present and future shame enters into the individual's decisions and behavior on a par with material costs and benefits of those actions.

The strategy of shaming clashes with a consideration that emotions may be triggered by beliefs about the motivations of others.[2] A policy of punishing offenders by 'shaming' risks being counterproductive since shaming may produce violent counter-actions. The tendency of action produced by shame is for the individual to hide or disappear; that of guilt, to make atonement or confess; in the case of envy and malice, to destroy. Both guilt and shame may provoke extreme and violent reactions, especially if considered unfair by the individual intended to be shamed or if the individual is made to feel guilty. Elster says, "Unlike the person who is in the grip of an acute emotion of shame or anger, people who are subject to an all-consuming durable passion are perfectly capable of acting in an instrumentally rational fashion."[3]

To feel envious is to feel inferior, so individuals may blame someone else for their situation. By this 'dissonance reduction' mechanism, the horrible feeling of

---

[2] Matthew Rabin. "Incorporating Fairness into Game Theory and Economics." *American Economic Review* 83 (1993) 1281-1302.
[3] Jon Elster. "Emotions and Economic Theory." *Journal of Economic Literature* 36 (1998) 47-74.

envious inferiority can be transmuted into the wonderful feeling of righteous indignation and playing upon the fear of shame or the fear of guilt in others.

Often worked with the 'why-question' by distrustful, malicious individuals, an effort to control others by provoking fear of guilt or fear of shame produces frustration and anger. The why-question cannot be answered which intensifies feelings of unfairness and either guilt or shame, or both. Both fear of guilt and fear of shame are sometimes utilized prominently by those individuals who are under stress of illness. They become accusative, blame-laying, shaming, chaotic, and distrustful.

These individuals seek the most defenseless, vulnerable members of the staff for their undermining tactics of shame and ridicule. Ridicule reduces the emotional burden of the ridiculer by arousing hate in the person ridiculed, at the same time neutralizing the power of the victim. Though always injurious, the injury caused by shame and ridicule increases as the culture tends to externalize sanctions of behavior. To lose one's good name in a shame culture is to lose one's right to existence, in this sense with the possibility that ridicule may be disastrous to the individual's self confidence or fatal to his existence within the group.[4]

The tactic of shaming or ridicule by a distrustful patient or family member is immensely distressing to the therapy staff, nurses and doctors. Its practitioners are particularly malicious and ill-willed. Such behavior may stimulate the rise of intense anger within the staff toward the patient or family member. Such malice stimulates the individual shamed or ridiculed to want to harm and destroy, but this reciprocal treatment can not be permitted when in a therapeutic situation. To maintain a professional manner and demeanor requires great self-control and self-assurance along with support of the entire staff.

Communication about the presence of shaming and guilt-provoking individuals is all-important in dealing with these distrustful individuals as with other members of the distrustful ranks. The importance of maintaining an even-handed approach to distrustful individuals cannot be overstated. When the distrustful perceive that their tactic is not having its expected effect, they will usually back away from it. If an angry reaction by a staff member occurs, the distrustful person has both won and lost: won in the sense of causing harm to a staff member, but has lost what they most need in the ability to work with the patient and family toward medical or rehabilitation goals.

The individual or individuals of the therapy staff, nurses, doctors, and others singled out by the shaming and guilt-provoking patients or family members may need the utmost of understanding and support by the rest of the staff. The effect of

---

[4] Elliott. p. 85.

shaming and guilt projected onto the staff by such individuals can be immensely traumatic, seen as unfair, and a severe test of the integrity of the therapy staff and the values and mutual nurturing of members of the staff. Those staff members who are victims of the shaming and guilt-provoking, distrustful individuals feel devastated and may be especially traumatized depending on which culture they themselves grew-up in. Most people will try to bear such insults and degradation alone and seek solitude when they most need comforting and companionship and support of their sympathetic fellow professionals.

Everyone experiences these distrustful and hateful individuals at some time in their careers. No greater therapy can be administered than to one another. Communication about the distrustful is obviously mandatory. The burden is too great for any one person to bear. Thus, the concept of the 'therapy team' has its greatest meaning.

B. "Thanks Anyway, Doc."

Like most internists, part of my practice is seeing healthy patients who request physical examinations which generally prove to be genteel encounters with interesting people. They return periodically for re-examination, and I noticed that patients that I know well and see socially sit by my desk, heart racing, palms sweating, and throat parched before a visit that usually is pleasant for me, if at times a little tedious and routine.

I have come to realize that the patient knows all too well that a check-up means facing the fearful unknown directly, and it has become apparent that there is no such thing as a "routine check-up." There is some reason this patient chose this particular time to face the possibility that something might be amiss. It may take extreme patience and the resources of Hercule Poriot, Sherlock Holmes, and Inspector Clouseau to find the reason, which may be apparent only in retrospect on discovering that a distant uncle or his wife's friend's neighbor has developed a dread malady.

Physicians have tried many ways to ease the tedium of the check-up, such as changing the name to interval examination, multiphasic examination, periodic examination, executive physical examination, or another euphemism. But a check-up is a check-up. Nor has the computer helped.

The economists in their criticisms of medicine suggest the check-up is not "cost effective." The cost of finding a case of tuberculosis with routine chest X-rays or a rectal cancer with a routine proctoscopic examination runs upward of $15,000 and, come to think of it, neither patient thanked me. We take pride in a meticulous examination and finding a subclinical disease— "picked up a heart murmur," and the patient says, "Now, can I get life insurance?"; "picked up a thyroid nodule," and the patient says, "Now, I suppose I will have to have surgery?"

The cost accountants and the econo-physicians say we shouldn't do "routine" examinations. Personally, I welcome the news. No more recitations of the litany of normal test results; no more ritual explaining why a new hypertensive patient must take a medication for life; no more exasperating diet instructions to the newly discovered, over-weight diabetic.

As I became more experienced, I found that I, too, faced the unknown when a patient appeared for a routine examination, and I lost some of my sense of ease and assurance of the past. Now, I'm a bit guarded and chary; a slight tremor in my handwriting, my throat a little dry. For example:

A man entered my office wearing a black golf shirt, red plaid slacks, and white leather running shoes. He shook my hand vigorously.

"How are ya, doc?"

He placed his billfold on the desk, on top of an insurance form, then neatly placed his sunglasses and car keys along side. He folded his hands across his lap and answered my inquiring the reason he interrupted his normal life cycle on the most beautiful day of the year to come to my office.

"Nothing. Feel great! Just want to make sure everything is okay. Actually, my wife made this appointment."

Now the flag is up, the chips are down. I tugged my collar as a few beads of moisture formed on my brow. I have learned from experience that this is my last chance, in a moment it will be too late.

"Usually, everything is as fine as it seems, but life is full of surprises. I never know where a check-up may lead."

He sat up abruptly, fumbled his keys in a moment of solemn concentration, sat immobile a long moment, then eased back in his chair, deciding to continue with it. Nothing good can come of this encounter for me except the lonely satisfaction that I have done a proper job. If he is well, we have appeased his spouse; if something abnormal turns up, all hell breaks loose. Small wonder that no patient has thanked me for finding something important that he or she didn't expect.

For several years running, such an insouciant gentleman appeared regularly for his annual check-ups, certain that it was all unnecessary as he felt well, sang regularly in the church choir, and played tennis daily. Since his son was a chiropractor, he took pleasure and some pains to bring me up to date on the modern wonders of the "healing profession," eroding any confidence or trust in this particular physician-patient relationship, since he was even more certain that neither the check-up nor I were necessary. The check-up, to him, was a talisman, like the atheist in church—just in case.

He offered a vague sensation, occurring only in certain infrequent circumstances, glowing with confidence that it was trivial and medically inexplicable. Further investigation demonstrated an abnormal exercise electrocardiogram, abnormal coronary angiograms, leading to coronary by-pass surgery at a prestigious university hospital of his choosing. I never saw him again, although some time later, I received a note enclosed with his statement that he went along with it to please his spouse, but that he was sure that it all, including the surgery, was unnecessary.

Another faithful and long-time patient kept his appointments regularly, although suspicious rumblings reached me that his wife questioned my professional competence, she had departed my practice some years previously. No new symptoms appeared and no bowel complaints could be elicited. On rectal examination, there was a tiny fold of mucosa that was slightly prominent, but not clearly abnormal. My patient, my friend, dressed while I struggled with the conflict of the cost effectiveness of a possibly needless proctoscopic examination, versus letting it pass, as it was probably unimportant. We discussed it, and I decided it was so small I would have a surgeon handle it.

The surgeon initially thought I was imagining things, a judgement I would gladly accept, then he found a tiny area to biopsy—rectal cancer in the tip of a tiny polyp, likely cured by this minor procedure alone. I naively expected that the patient and his wife would congratulate me and gratefully acknowledge my skill and percipience. What followed was an ugly complaint about my nominal fee, and an abrupt change of physicians.

The residual carry-over of the check-up is even more treacherous as we hear of patients who drop dead outside their doctor's office after a satisfactory annual examination and negative test results. For example, a woman I had known for years, six months after examination, attended a lecture on self-examination of the breast. That night, she discovered a small nodule in her breast that proved to be malignant. There followed accusations and calumny that it should have been discovered six months previously at her check-up, even though these tumors may double in size every two weeks, and she did not return.

A young woman that I had known since her adolescence, developed abdominal pain, went to an emergency room at a nearby city, and at surgery, a large ovarian cyst was found, which can develop rapidly. The last I saw of her was in a department store, where she loudly informed me that I had "missed it." I was surprised at my presence of mind when I reminded her that her exam was eight months earlier and the pelvic exam was performed a few weeks before that at the Student Health Center of her beloved university and alma mater. No matter, someone, probably an intern, planted the words "missed it" to trump-up his or her own image, and the subject was no longer open to reason.

So, you see, dear healthcare economist, cost-accountant, managed care advocate and zealot, I, too, have grave concerns about the wisdom of the check-up, but for entirely different reasons. Your dark and sinister motivations frighten me; mine are those of the jungle—survival!

After residency, like many physicians, I practiced my newly acquired skills, my profession as an officer and a gentleman in the United States Air Force. My trench, duty station, battle post, or excubitorium was designated "Sick Call." A staff sergeant of no outstanding features presented himself for a check-up. His symptoms were vague and nondescript, a review of his intricate bodily functions proved that they were performing harmoniously in their respective internal and external milieus, psycho-social environment, and efficiently extracting from the input and dejecting a proper output, leaving a slightly corpulent, nondescript staff sergeant with no outstanding features.

I turned my attention to the corpus and found the bodily orchestra equally harmonious, if a bit dull in the treble, slightly flat in the bass, and a broad middle range, with a rhythm that was monotonously in step. He dressed. I clasped his shoulder and dispatched him on laboratory rounds of sophisticated technical equipment that clicked and whirred, jiggled and teased his vital juices, and recorded his galvanic aura.

He returned to her "the news" a few days later. The news was that his results were nondescript, negative, no abnormality noted, within normal limits, and didn't vary from the textbook description of the perfect airman by so much as a tenth of a standard deviation.

I was at my best. With calm and confidence, I committed my precious and hard-earned, if tenuous, reputation by saying that he was, in my opinion, as of that moment, in no uncertain terms, cost-efficiently healthy.

Silence.

I placed my black USAF ballpoint pen on his manila USAF chart, sat back, folded my arms across my white USAF coat. He sat, starring out the window. Snow fell on the Chugach Mountains. He slowly, absently, shifted his gaze to me, leaned forward, hands on knees, and said, "Is that it?"

I again affirmed my opinion as to his state of health, expressed relief upon receiving favorable test results, of resources well-spent, and suggested that he might even live a long and healthy life in retirement.

He stood. As he left my office, he said, "Well, doc, thanks anyway."

His sky-blue, cerulean, ungainly military presence retrogressed down the long, gray hallway. I watched with a mixture of confusion and anger. Visions of managed care to come. "Some gratitude," I said to myself, but wait, wait! "I'll take it! I'll take it!" This perversion of trust. A draw is the best I can expect.

C. SPLITTERS AND SQUATTERS

Splitters are one of the most potentially devastating individuals that appear on our Rehabilitation Unit. They are out to do harm, to destroy the workings of the Unit and to destroy individuals of the therapy staff. Deftly, they go about turning members of the staff against one another. They are distrust in pure culture. Subtle and deceitful, they undermine trust, destroy confidence, and subtly traumatize the unwary.

Since these patients stay on the Unit a number of days, they get to know the nursing and therapy staff fairly well. Splitters seek conflicting information, or interpret instructions as conflicting, from one staff member to turn against another. They confront one with the conflicting instructions of another, or they shade or distort what has been said or advised or done. Disorder and chaos are their element. In chaos they find comfort and a sense of power. In the discomfort of others they find satisfaction and an outlet for their perverse aggression.

If conflicting information does not come to them spontaneously, they stimulate and confabulate contradictory instructions. "But nurse X told me to do this and nurse Y something else," or "therapist A disagrees with therapist B." So angry and threatening are the Splitters at times that the staff may opt to ignore the Splitter, or to take the side of the Splitter against others of the staff rather than to face the emotional storm of the Splitter.

In one particularly pernicious example, a patient graded each nurse and therapist giving each a report everyday, which this patient took the utmost glee and enjoyment in causing embarrassment and uneasiness in the staff member confronted. The result was many hurt feelings and eventually mutual distrust.

So injurious and undermining are the Splitters that the staff comes to distrust each other and may work against each other without knowing about the other staff member who has also been demeaned. Those staff members so treated also tend to bear their injury silently rather than conferring with other staff personnel in an open discussion.

The first priority is to protect the members of the staff and then to identify and evaluate what the Splitter is doing. Confront the Splitter as soon as possible. The longer it goes on, the more distrustful and difficult the situation is to deal with, and staff morale can be expected to suffer. Once out in the open, members of the staff may become angry and resentful toward the Splitter, which is quite understandable under the circumstances. By knowing what the Splitter is doing, the staff maintains its integrity, both personally and professionally.

Once the Splitter has been exposed and the staff understands the situation, the destructive efforts of the Splitter collapse without harm. On occasion, the Splitter reinforces his or her efforts and must be confronted which may be a very disagreeable interaction. The Splitter must be handled carefully and not by reciprocal affect, but informed in a non-threatening way what the staff has observed and that it will not be tolerated. It is not a time for analysis or sympathy, but deftly asserting the principles of the Unit, to care for each patient to the best of our abilities, and the Splitters cooperation is necessary.

The Squatter

The Squatter refuses to get out of bed. They may claim that they distrust the staff, but in fact they may have a number of motivations, not the least is, like the Splitter, intent on controlling the nurses and therapy staff and causing discord and disorganization. Threatening and accusing, the Squatters consider themselves entitled to do whatever they wish whenever they wish to do it. Undermining trust is their method, and most any ruse may be tried. The vehicle for their distrust is anger; sometimes sullenness, and occasionally vituperation.

The Squatter refuses to take responsibility for himself or herself. Participating in their therapy sessions may be denigrated into play, or a sport, or a game they don't like. Testing the will of the therapy staff, the Squatters are passive intimidators, or passive bullies who are sometimes socially inept

"No-option therapy" means that they participate or they leave. Some would protest that insisting the patient give up inalienable individual rights is opposed to patient's rights, but to allow a Squatter to squat rather than do what is prescribed to permit them to regain independence cannot be condoned and still remain on an active Rehabilitation Unit.

Seldom does the impasse reach a critical point, although reason is of little help. The Squatter knows what we are trying to accomplish for them, but acting negative and passively aggressive is their style of behavior. No time for sympathy or analysis, but time to get up and get on with it. We call it 'Leadership from the Rear,' just short of using an electric cattle prod.

At the opposite extreme is the patient who refuses to leave the hospital or the Rehab Unit when their stay is completed. The realities of insurance payment for their hospitalization can be called into play, if necessary. A Letter of Denial of further coverage from the hospital's Utilization Committee usually convinces the Squatter or the Squatter's family. The truly crafty protest to Utilization Committees, gaining a few more days.

Eventually, most conflicts with Squatters and Splitters resolve without excessive strife. They represent a small portion of the two per cent that consume the most energy and time to deal with. Families may be enlisted to encourage the patient, or families may work against rehabilitation efforts. We usually have forewarning of the family's willingness to cooperate or support the medical staff efforts.

I'm told that eviction is possible as last resort; I have never called upon anyone to be evicted, although I have come close to it. Squatters may test one's creative abilities to deal with the distrustful, but the challenge is often not as great as it may appear at first. Communication among the staff members is essential, so that a united effort is presented to the Squatter. Social Services are especially creative in dealing with Squatters, though some Squatters are major problems.

D. THE ALTERNATIVE MEDICINE PARRY

The distrustful individual who places little trust in medical professionals is a ready and willing mark for the alternative medicine practitioners, where like meets like. When forced in one way or another into contact with the medical profession, doctors, nurses, and hospitals, they are already distrustful. Alternative medicines present a chance for them to cast doubt on standard medical care. Criticism of treatment plans for problem patients may be authoritatively claimed by advocates of alternative or non-traditional therapies.

The reason they are alternative treatments and not whatever is standard of practice of medicine is that they are supported by subjective opinion and not by clinical research or rational medical practice. Since alternative therapies can neither be proved nor disproved, and comparative data are absent, then by *argumentum ad ignorantiam*, whatever hasn't been proven to be false is considered true, they may claim more than can be rationally justified.

Alternative medicine, with its anti-establishment, anti-intellectual stance, becomes 'institutionalized distrust' used by its adherents as a wedge between patient and doctor.

The alternative medicine-mindset of the distrustful can be a most frustrating, energy expending, and time consuming effort in working with a committed alternative medicine devotee. Their *modus vivendi* is to distrust, to undermine, to subvert while accepting no responsibility. Especially active are family members who insist on trying a root or grain or brew of something or other that requires a doctor's approval. No thanks.

A 'Pain Society' provides a ready and willing market that is composed of members of a gullible, affluent public who seek out alternative practitioners promising immediate relief. "Infallable," "speedy," and "permanent" are tenets of the alternative medical providers today as it was for the charlatans of the nineteenth century. Few questions are asked by either the public or alternative practitioners, and little is given in return. Nostrums abound promising great things but delivering nothing in the way of actual results. Although the nineteenth century is considered the heyday of quackery, the end of the twentieth century saw a vigorous comeback of the nostrum trade.

Alternative medicine appeals to the gullible, the distrustful, and anti-establishment population: a large population since over half of respondents to surveys admit to using alternative treatments, the economic consequences are immense. Healthy individuals who are well but want to feel better are easy prey, even though I claim it is difficult to make someone with no complaints feel better. As observed by others, university towns are hotbeds of quackery and alternative medicine practitioners. Those who know a great deal about one thing, Greek literature or quantum physics, don't necessarily know about medicine or those who sell alternative medicines.

In the nineteenth century, Oliver Wendell Holmes referred to "toadstool millionaires" whose exaggerated claims were met with a shrug, a chuckle or a sigh, and were often thought of as quaint, comical, and harmless with little social stigma. Will Rogers said of the claimed healing powers of the Claremore wells that a legless man took the waters and "went away a Centipede." Hadacol, laetrile, chelation, Krebiozen, copper bracelets, the diet industry, aloe vera, St. John's Wort, the list grows. Physicians in the practice of medicine do not worship at an altar where "no strange fires ever burn," but are confronted by the devoted alternative practitioners or 'providers' of distrust and a false hope.[5]

A parallel development with alternative medicine occurred in the research science environment in academia and the growth of 'postmodernism' which rejects the principle of reason of the Enlightenment, and denies the possibility of objective knowledge. Over the past three decades, universities were infiltrated by critics of learning, intellectual rigor, and empirical evidence who "pass off

---

[5] James Harvey Young. *American Health Quackery* Princeton, NJ: Princeton University Press, 1992; James Harvey Young. *The Medical Messiahs: A Social History of Health Quackery in Twentieth-Century America*. Princeton, NJ: Princeton University Press, 1967.

political opinion as science and engage in bogus scholarship." Alternative medicine, similarly, must be considered anti-intellectual, anti-medicine, and misplaced trust.

Not long before she died, anthropologist Margaret Mead cautioned that the United States was entering "a new Dark Ages of medieval mysticism and mumbo-jumbo, of belief based on self-interest, mob politics, and fear rather than research and open-minded inquiry," which is congruous with the rise of alternative medicine, "A brand of anti-intellectualism is running amok..."[6]

Mathematician Norman Levitt is more sardonic in the matter of conditions within the world of academia: "Windbags, bluffers, and moral one-uppers are having a field day. The daft and the silly are raised on high."[7] Even more remarkable is the commonality of the ineffectiveness of science departments in academia with physicians to counter their critics. The timidity and inability of most scientists and scientific societies to rebuff attacks condemns the feebleness of their attempts to understand the attacks, and to oppose them.[8]

Alternative medicine interferes with treatment plans of medical professionals, and some are hazardous with dangerous interactions with regular medicines. Medical professionals don't know everything, but it's still the way to bet. The distrust inherent in alternative medicine in the rehabilitation setting or treatment of chronic diseases is difficult to control, but the phenomenon is as old as mankind and must be understood by medical practitioners, who must also understand it as the way of the world for a great number of patients and their families, largely based on distrust of ethical medical practice, or misplaced trust in alternative medicine.

"When reason sleeps, the monsters of human pride, foolishness, malice, and cruelty emerge to do their worst."[9]

---

[6] William A. Henry, III. *In Defense of Elitism*. New York, London, Toronto: Doubleday, 1994. p. 3.

[7] Norman Levitt. "Mathematics as the Stepchild of Contemporary Culture." in *The Flight From Science and Reason*. Paul R. Gross, Norman Levitt, & Martin W. Lewis, editors. *Annals of New York Academy of Science*. vol. 775. 1996. p. 48.

[8] Gerald Holton. "Science Education and the Sense of Self." in *The Flight From Science and Reason*. Paul R. Gross, Norman Levitt, & Martin W. Lewis, editors. *Annals of New York Academy of Science*. vol. 775. 1996. p. 552.

[9] Paul R. Gross and Norman Levitt. *Higher Superstition: The Academic Left and Its Quarrels with Science*. Baltimore and London: Johns Hopkins University Press, 1994. p. 215.

E. THE ABSOLUTIST

Medical explanations to patients and families almost always require a discussion of prognosis, i.e. foreknowledge, or forecasting. More officially, from *Blakiston's New Gould Medical Dictionary*, prognosis is defined: "A prediction of the duration, course, and termination of a disease, based on all information available in the individual case and knowledge of how the disease behaves generally."

To the Absolutist, prognosis becomes a guarantee, a certainty, concrete nut-and-bolts reality, a promise of the future that the doctor was expected to foretell and promised to deliver. One of the 'Rules' of business says, "forecasting is a difficult thing, particularly as it deals with the future." An organizations of economists awards "Forecaster of the Year" to the economist who had the best predictions for the previous year: no economist has won it twice suggesting a randomness in the award.

Perhaps in times past, doctors or lawyers or bankers, could make absolute statements about the future, no doubt risking life and limb in the case that his or her prediction of the future fell short of what was 'promised.' With the application of statistical methods to biology in the early twentieth century, and later to medicine, absolute prognostics gave way to biometrics, which measured variations in biology. Statistical variation in the course and outcome of diseases entered medical practice in the mid-twentieth century. But not to the Absolutist!

Never mind the inconstancy and inconsistency of human existence, the Absolutist is after concrete, positive *answers*. The Absolutist is an intellectual hold-over from the eighteenth and nineteenth centuries when popular opinion held that all could be known and everything could be predicted like wheels turning in a giant mechanical universe.

A ninety per cent chance of a recovery is like a red-flag to an enraged bull to the Absolutist. That a promise of the future is expressed as a *possibility* or *probability* instead of a *certainty* kindles passions in the Absolutist. A sarcastic reply follows, "Well, I know that medicine is an *inexact* science." Emphasis on 'inexact' destroys the possibility of the establishment of trust.

By the fallacy of *argumentum ignoratiam* (what isn't known for certain to be true is false) the Absolutist satisfies himself or herself that trust is not possible. The Absolutist is sure that the circle has been squared, that mathematics and physics are concrete and far ahead of all other intellectual endeavors, and that the doctors are holding out on them. A relative world is a hostile place of existence to the Absolutist.

Demand of the Absolutist for certain knowledge is a throwback to primitive behavior, and they resort to equally primitive behavior in their conviction that life is constant warfare between each individual against everyone else. The law of the jungle. Even the best of science has a subjective aspect to it; not all of the results of science come from cold, factual calculation or measurement. Solid matter, like the floor we walk on, is more like a statistical behavior of a mass of bees or atoms than what appears to perfectly solid concrete.

In the event of a confrontation with an Absolutist, I take the advantage at once! I say, "All sciences are inexact. Exactness of science ended in the late nineteenth century with relativity. Mathematics is by definition an approximation, and that physics is the most inexact of all sciences. Only the illusion of exactness persists."

Not welcome intelligence to the Absolutist. It's a promise or guarantee they want, so they will be free of anxiety about the nature of the patient's illness and what is to be expected of them. The Absolutist allows no compromise with reality. If the Absolutist comprehends or accepts the modern Law of Uncertainty, they become a little sheepish or head down or duck out. Too bad. They lost their advantage and stump.

Nevertheless, on occasion, trust ensues. At least a measure of half-hearted trust. If they do not comprehend the notion of statistical uncertainty, further explanation is not productive and we must do the best we can under the circumstances. While the idea of a concrete reality persists with the Absolutist, that something else or a rival concept has been introduced may be all that is necessary. At least, the anger and hostility are moderated to a workable level.

Chapter 6

FUTILITY

A. INFORMED CONSENT: "YOU'RE THE DOCTOR." BOUNDED RATIONALITY

A long-time patient came to my office for advice about a technical therapeutic procedure. Since we had known each other for some years, exchange of views was free of any social or professional encumbrance. I expressed my views of the options open to him, medically, surgically or by any other means. After a lengthy explanation during which I knew he comprehended, we discussed the basic nature of the problem, and the potential benefits and potential hazards and risks as well as options of other therapies or no therapy.

When we concluded our discussion, he said, "You're the doctor, you tell me what I should do."

I was dismayed that after so long a discussion and such an exacting explanation the decision would be put back to me when I had taken great efforts to fully inform him in an honest manner. Why had I devoted so much time and energy and patience to end where I thought I had started? Surely, I had accomplished more than this. My entire education and training and experience brought to bear on this essential, personal medical encounter.

Then, I thought that his was the best response possible. He had the information he needed, and he trusted my opinion. I had greater respect for him, not less.

In working with professionals that I confer with over personal matters, such as attorneys, accountants, insurance agents, etc., I often think of this encounter. I can't possibly know as much as the professionals that I consult, nor can patients possibly know as much as I know about medical issues they consult about with me.

The essential ingredient is trust, no matter what alarmed ethicists may say. We all operate in what the psychologists call 'bounded rationality': that even with the best and most complete information, and even if we act as rationally as we are able, we can't possibly know everything about a complex issue, and we can't always act completely in a rational manner.[1]

When I speak with a real estate agent, I will never understand the complexities of a 'wrap-around mortgage.' I must trust him or her to some extent. When my personal attorney explains the intricacies of estate planning, I may get the basics of it, but eventually I must trust him. When my financial manager describes the dismaying options available about bonds, arbitrage and other arcane financial workings, I must trust that he or she knows what he or she is doing.

As important as trust is the conviction that if a personal adviser doesn't gain my trust by his or her explanations, even though I can't possibly comprehend it fully, I must be free to go to someone else without fear or regret. Both of us are better off. And, so it is between patient and physician, the same applies.

Logical thought and sensible behavior is not the norm for many people most of the time, and all people are less than rational at some time or another. The adage that all of the people can be fooled some of the time and some people can be fooled all of the time, but all people cannot be fooled all of the time rings true today. The use of logic distinguishes between correct and incorrect reasoning, which is both art and science. Mistakes in reasoning, or fallacies, are as important to recognize as correct reasoning.[2] We are implored by 'spin' to think incorrectly and illogically, to lower our sense of right, to do the will of the 'spin doctors.'

The study of logic is far beyond the scope of this volume, but an awareness of the methods of some practitioners of deceit is essential. Discrediting the present to direct the individual's focus on a vague, distant and glorious future attracts the disaffected and distrustful. Undermining established norm and institutions, discrediting those in authority by the fallacies of *General Corruption*, *Imputation of Bad Design*, or *Imputation of Bad Motives* is reported daily in the news. Illogic and 'spin' has its effect by endless repetition of dubious claims to destroy trust. The manipulation of the public by bogus individuals occurs by the *Fallacy of Self-*

---

[1] Herbert A. Simon. "Introductory Comment." in Herbert A. Simon, with Massimo Egidi, Robin Marris and Riccardo Viale. *Economics, Bounded Rationality and the Cognitive Revolution* Brookfield, VT: Edward Elgar, 1992, pp. 3-7.
[2] Irving M. Copi. *Introduction to Logic*. New York and London: Macmillan, 1968.

Assumed Authority.[3] The most illogical claim will be believed and acted upon if repeated often enough. A charismatic leader works his or her spell by techniques of propaganda that may be outlandish but wins adherents nevertheless. Emotional tirades are their means of operation; undermining trust is their stock in trade.[4]

The effect of destroying trust is especially prevalent in mass behavior, or the behavior of crowds. Those who would influence the individual to their own cause, to undermine trust, appeal to the subconscious rather than to logical, reasonable conscious thought, and work towards the lowest common denominator. Nor can the individual depend on prominent people to exercise good judgment and reason at certain times. Le Bon, a nineteenth-century French physician and crowd psychologist, says, "a gathering of scientific men or of artists, owing to the mere fact that they form an assemblage, will not deliver judgments on general subjects sensibly different from those rendered by a gathering of masons or grocers."[5]

Fear and hate, jealousy and envy are the fodder of demagogues, whether political, religious, business, or others that unite individuals to a cause. The obstacle they must overcome is trust in reason and trust in established institutions, and at the same time, transfer allegiance to the goals of their cause at the expense of the individual by emotional, irrational claims, no matter what they profess. Perpetual awareness and heightened caution prepares individuals for the treachery and deceit of those whose purpose is to undermine trust and transfer allegiance to institutions and movements which the individual may not appreciate at first. In fact, the initial arguments put forth by demagogues is especially noted for its illogic and irrationality. By force of personality and emotional harangues producing fear, fired by hate, repeated endlessly, reasonable behavior may be subverted into destructive behavior: the working of the crowd towards distrust and misplaced allegiance.

The same process is at work in clinical settings. Some individuals, by the same techniques as the demagogues, sabotage trust, placing a barrier between patient and therapy staff. Similarly, constant awareness of the possibility and measures to counter distrust become important to treatment of individual patients.

---

[3] Jeremy Bentham. *Bentham's Book of Political Fallacies*. editor Harold A. Larrabee. Baltimore: The Johns Hopkins Press, 1952.
[4] Eric Hoffer. *The True Believer: Thoughts on the Nature of Mass Movements*. New York: Harper & Row, 1951, pp. 66-73.
[5] Gustave Le Bon. *The Crowd: A Study of the Popular Mind*. Dunwoody, GA: Norman S. Berg, 2nd ed. 1984, p. 171.

B. Personality Conflict

Conflicts with certain patients are inevitable, given the stress of medical encounters, enormous range of people, and uncertainty in medical practice. An elderly patient came to my office some years ago accompanied by her daughter. The patient sat in the chair next to my examining table and scowled at me for the entire duration of the visit, never saying a word. Her daughter did the talking. Even when directly questioned, the patient had little to say, usually remaining completely mum. Her hostile, distrustful facial expression never changed and her unprovoked hostility never abated.

I did my best to engage the patient in to the merest of responses and tried in every way to be friendly and to show interest in her medical care. No way.

At subsequent visits, she seemed to enter the room angry and distrustful, and remained so throughout the session. Her daughter indicated no dissatisfaction with my care and the two reliably returned to her appointments on time. She followed advice and took her medicines as prescribed.

After a time, her daughter came in without her mother, the patient. She handed my receptionist a Transfer of Records authorization. She was going to a new physician.

The daughter asked to speak with me, which I greeted with some foreboding. She said that she was sorry to change doctors, but her mother thought we had a 'personality conflict.' I was puzzled in that she seldom said a word during her visits to my office. Certainly no difficult words came between us.

Nevertheless, she may be right. I, too, am on the taciturn side. It seems that we are most likely to not 'get along' with those who are most like ourselves. My closest patients and easiest rapport is with those who are more voluble and outgoing, which they reciprocate.

So, don't fight it. Recognize it. Gaining the trust of those most like ones self may be the most difficult. We can't be all things to all people.

Some say it is a form of 'self-hate,' which is more analytic than I care for here. One projects dissatisfactions in one's self to someone who resembles us and we dislike or hate our dissatisfactions in them. Recognizing this peculiarity of human nature early may save a great deal of stress and consternation later. It is not a time to gain trust easily.

Changing doctors or therapists may not be so easy in the Rehabilitation Unit, but the doctor or therapist or nurse may be saved anger and self-reproach by recognizing this facet of human nature. In some instances, the two like-individuals can work together. Sometimes, it is better to cut one's losses and move on. Most of all, a working relationship is a two-way street. The patient must be willing and able to establish a trusting relationship with the therapy team. By being aware of the possibility of conflict, much aggravation and wasted energy can be prevented, and morale maintained.

C. THE DOONEY-BOURKE BOUNDRY

Not long after the Christmas Holidays, a Family Conference was held for a patient who was an older man and still employed; his wife and three middle age daughters attended. The patient, a kindly gentleman who had provided for the stylish expectations of the womenfolk of the family had worked hard all of his adult life but not to any great financial gain. He asked little for himself, and worked diligently at all of his therapy sessions hoping to please everyone he came in contact with–nurses, therapists, doctors and everyone who came onto the Rehabilitation Unit.

At the Family Conference, the four women's chairs were evenly arranged in a properly straight line. Resting on the floor in front of each was a brand new Dooney-Bourke handbag of wonderfully elegant leather and brilliant brass fittings, with its logo out-facing. The Dooney-Bourkes were placed on the floor broadside to the staff as if each was a bunker, bullet proof, shock proof, and unassailable: like the crenels and merlons atop the Tower of London, boiling oil ready to be cast down on a rebellious multitude below.

Each of the four women wore matching outfits, not to be further described, but to say that they were neatly tailored and no doubt blessed by fashion apostles. Their hair equally regulation, or GI, perfectly arranged, combed and 'blown-out.' Topping it all were matching unsmiling botoxed faces that gave no clue.

Take a look. There they were, in perfect alignment. In perfect control. A defense to stop the Pentagon or the Packers or a Sherman tank. In the history of warfare, it resembled the Maginot Line in France during World War I. Dug-in trenches. Artillery thundering overhead. Bunkers and concrete gun emplacements. Firing away month after month. No quarter asked. No quarter given. No prisoners. No apology. No gain. No trust.

The Family Conference went about as one would expect. The patient did not attend. The four women sat rather stiffly and spoke terse words in abrupt remarks. They did not want to hear anything that might abase their ideas of continuation of material favor and to challenge their right to fashion and sense of style. Cooperation with the therapy staff was guarded and whatever involvement they may agree to in continued care at home would be on their terms with the least intrusion into their daily routines and avoiding all inconveniences.

After the conference, we had a sense that we had accomplished little for our patient and that he faced a bleak future. His disability was too great and his age against him that he would ever be able to return to gainful employment or very much independence. Nevertheless, we did as much as possible to enlist as much family involvement as we were able. The discharge process went forward with little sense of satisfaction within the therapy staff. The Dooney-Bourke Boundary could not be breached. In follow-up after the patient had gone home, the family kept a distance from being involved with a patient who was not wholly functional. Nevertheless, the recommended assistance was hired and life went on. Unsmiling, unfeeling, unsatisfying.

The Dooney-Bourke Boundry is not a place to die against. Some situations are irremediable. Recognize it quickly, or be destroyed without ceremony. (Boiling oil is prepared and waiting.) Our responsibility to patients goes on despite reluctance of the distrustful and unengaged families. At the same time, contain your losses. Don't expect gratitude. Any trust gained will be hard-won.

D. DISGUST LEADS TO DISTRUST

Disgust is a basic emotion characterized by a certain facial expression, an inappropriate action, a distinctive physiological manifestation, and a characteristic feeling-state of revulsion. It is manifested by closing the nares of the nose and opening the mouth which symbolically closes off the offensive odor, and gaping which allows contents of the mouth to run out. Disgust may lead to distrust, or a manifestation of distrust. The mixture of the idea of the object of disgust and "bad taste" motivations is termed *offensive*. The focus on oral incorporation distinguishes disgust from other emotions.

A negative attitude toward incorporation into the body is characteristic of both disgust and danger. Disgust and nausea are closely related, though nausea is not necessary nor a sufficient condition for disgust. Aversion is a general feeling of disgust but limited to the mouth plus odor for distaste, and nausea is a much more prominent concomitant of disgust than of distaste. The mouth serves as an emotional, highly charged border between self and non-self.

By the 'omnivore's dilemma,' the vital importance of nutrition and severe risks of poisoning may together account for the strong affective responses associated with this process. The conflict represented by the opposing tendencies to both fear and to explore new foods, or to like both familiar and novel foods leads to *ambivalence*. Objects of disgust, though offensive, are almost all animal in origin and at the same time nutritious.

The prospect of consuming things contacted by people who are disliked or viewed as unsavory often elicits disgust. Disgust varies across cultures, but most always contains body waste products, yet it is not objects but contexts that are disgusting. *Anomalous* items, such as those that are unique or those that simultaneously contain properties of different classes, are disturbing and hence become the objects of taboo or pollution.

Anomalous items represent disorder, matter out of place, or 'dirt.' Viscous substances thought to be disgusting or polluting occupy an uncertain position between liquid and solid. Feces and other bodily excretions are ambiguous as to whether or not they are part of the self, also, challenges the live–dead dichotomy since feces represents the primary disgust-substance. The finding of excrement of a highly disturbed or agitated patient may call forth a dramatic outpouring of disgust by a visitor.

Psychological contamination occurs when people's response to physical contamination may have occurred. By the phenomenon of *Contamination and the Laws of Sympathetic Magic Contagion*, 'once in contact, always in contact,' or 'things which have once been in contact with each other continue ever afterwards to act on each other' leads to the psychological manifestation that a part is equal to the whole: or similarity in that 'like produces like,' or the image is equal to the object. Contagion and similarity account for the belief in 'action at a distance,' a fundamental feature of contamination. 'Sympathetic magic' of similarity and contagion holds that harming an image of a person [similarity] or a residue of a person, such as fingernail clippings [contagion] can harm the actual person, which is also called *backward causation*. Trust is impossible under these circumstances.

The laws of 'sympathetic magic' center on and highlight *personal contamination* and the role of interpersonal factors in disgust. The essential aspects of personal contamination are (1) The nature of the person contacting, and (2) The nature of the contact. *Contamination in Danger and Disgust* occurs with dangerous as well as with disgusting objects, which leads to *fear* in disgust that is harmful to the psyche, as opposed to the body.

Limits of Contamination: or Getting Along in a Physically Contaminated World requires some acknowledgement of imperfection of surroundings and a reasonable tolerance. Suspicion of contamination leads to distrust and avoidance of many substances. Avoiding contemplation of contamination possibilities is the more common solution. Closing one's eyes is a fundamental coping strategy seemingly absolutely necessary for dealing with a largely irrational and potentially overwhelming set of beliefs and attitudes about disgust. *Positive*

Contamination, the opposite of disgust, implies an asymmetry in the nature of contamination; negative events tend to be more salient and to be responded to with greater intensity than positive events.

Disgust provides a powerful way to transmit cultural values. Disgust is not present at birth and does not occur below age 8 years of age. The shared facial expression in distaste manifested by children suggests an origin of disgust in distaste, and subsequent distrust. The main features are *Primary disgusts*: feces and toilet training, or unconditioned stimulus or a conditioned stimulus. *Secondary disgusts*, like Pavlovian conditioning, results from spatially and/or temporally contingent association of a neutral substance with a disgust substance. Because disgust critically involves things foreign to the self, these intimate relations may weaken disgust by blurring the self-other distinction. Disgust and some instances of distrust seem primitive and irrational, yet they are products of a culture that is both uniquely human and apparently absent in children.[6]

Disgust readily translates to distrust and is often confused with distrust. A patient that is severely impaired, incontinent, etc. may provoke disgust in family members or visitors. Managing the disgust elements of medical care can be as challenging and any other aspect of Rehabilitation. Even giving simple injections to some family members may provoke aversion and a sensation of disgust. The Sybarite is especially adept at avoidance, but in some instances a Sybarite will come through, but usually when avoidance leads to greater expense in providing attendants and home health aids. Careful explanations and hands-on care by an attendant or family member reduces the problem of disgust.

E. PILLAR TO POST: FROM THE BORDERLINE AND BEYOND

A great amount of literature has been written about the borderline patient. Here, I deal only with the recognition of the problem and suggestions for management.[7]

The borderline personality is characterized by a pervasive instability of affect and interpersonal relationships, marked impulsiveness, with a high frequency of co-morbid anxiety and mood disorders. Subject to repetitive self-destructive behaviors and substance use disorders, the borderline individual may be difficult,

---

[6] Paul Rozin and April E. Fallon. "A Perspective on Disgust." *Psychological Review* 94 (1987) 23-41.

[7] Gross, Raz, et al. "Borderline Personality Disorder in Primary Care." *Archive of Internal Medicine* 162 (2002) 53-60; *DSM IV* American Psychiatric Association; Glen O. Gabbard. "*Borderline Personality Disorder: A Clinical Guide.*" Author John G. Gunderson. Washington, DC: American Psychiatric Press, 2001. Book review. *New England Journal of Medicine* 345 (2001 1003).

demanding, manipulative, non-complaint, disruptive, and certainly challenging. The pattern of unstable, intense interpersonal relationships alternates between idealization and devaluation. Affective instability with marked reactivity of mood shifts rapidly from baseline to depression, irritability, or anxiety, which lasts a few hours to a few days. Sudden mood changes and impulsiveness typify their relationships resulting in unstable, yet intense interpersonal relationships. They may seem intact one day and in extreme psychological distress the next.

Chronic feelings of emptiness or boredom plague their pursuit of happiness with frantic efforts to avoid abandonment. Persistent and markedly disturbed, distorted or unstable self-image and/or sense of self underlies their impulsive, affective liability, i.e. he or she may feel that they don't exist or that they embody evil. Identity disturbances are manifested as uncertainty about self-image, sexual orientation, long-term goals or career choice, type of friends desired, and preferred values. Transient, stress-related, severe dissociative experiences or paranoid ideation may precipitate inappropriate, intense anger or lack of control of anger, frequent displays of temper, constant anger, or recurrent combative episodes.

These patients may greet you with a highly emotional objection, or an angry complaint. Angry and intolerant, they react at extremes in most all situations. Every situation becomes a crisis, for they are highly trusting and highly distrusting, and at the same time, they are unable to moderate between extremes. Borderline individuals tend toward impulsiveness in at least two areas that are potentially self-damaging: spending, sex, substance use, shoplifting, reckless driving, binge eating, etc.

The borderline individual may seem charming, composed and in control one day raising hopes of being able to help themselves only to have hopes dashed, for the next day they are in despair, impulsive, emotionally labile, and frantic. Hatred and contempt directed towards those who try to help them leads to exasperation in the helpers and therapy team. Some medical workers have advised involvement of multiple clinicians to defuse the intensity of the borderline individual's emotional outbursts.

Since the borderline individual constantly test limits, establishing limits and holding to them is essential. Strangely, once limits are set, the borderline individual often obeys meekly, that which they so strongly objected to, and what they most stridently provoke.

Recognizing a borderline individual is most important, which is often associated with a visceral reaction and a sense of revulsion in the staff, which is a clue to dealing with a borderline patient.

About half of patients who are at the borderline are not recognized as having emotional or mental health problems and have received no mental health treatment. Intervention or meliorating the borderline patient is an enormous, prolonged task to be undertaken only by skilled mental health professionals and dedicated institutions. Once considered untreatable, a 'multimodal' strategy has been recommended for the borderline patient, with multiple clinicians involved to dilute the intensity of the borderline individual's counter-transference. Family intervention is also recommended.

Physicians may, in time, be able to establish rapport, feel less frustrated, and have a useful therapeutic effect by continually stressing interest and concern to the borderline patient. However, physicians and other members of the therapy team are cautioned not to get too close to these patients. Strike a balance between empathic recognition of the patient's fear of abandonment, with clear limit-setting on their behavior. Acknowledge the patient's strong feelings, but at the same time insist on appropriate behavior. Avoid responding to their provocations; try to remain emotionally neutral in what is often a highly charged situation.

Consider scheduling brief, structured, frequent visits that keeps the patient in touch with the therapy team, but keep the sessions brief to avoid excessive demands on the staff. Provide clear, non-technical answers to counter their scary, frightening fantasies and anxieties.

In the case of women patients, male physicians are strongly advised to have a female nurse present when conducting all physical examinations.

Coordinate care with mental health care professionals and other coworkers to avoid problems of splitting of the staff by the patient who may provoke opposition of one physician against another.

Discuss your feelings with colleagues. The behavior of borderline patients complicates diagnosis and treatment of depression and anxiety, and may mask a bipolar disorder, which should be in the hands of mental health specialists.

Complicating working with the borderline patient, hatred and contempt may be directed towards those who try to help them, leading to 'counter-transference' and feelings of exasperation and helplessness in the helpers. The term 'boundary violation' by patients, who test the limits of the therapeutic environment, is a useful concept. Patients have no professional code of ethics to be adhered to; they must have their battles which "clears the air" briefly, until the next time.

In the meantime, the borderline patient must be dealt with often in difficult therapeutic situations not of their choosing. Attempt to accomplish as much as possible within the limits of the current problem.

Don't analyze. Don't expect gratitude. A draw is a worthwhile notable accomplishment.

Chapter 7

REHAB MILIEU

A. EMILY'S HAIR

The morning our Rehabilitation Unit opened, within an hour of receiving our first patient, an elderly woman was admitted who the week before was seriously ill and had been ordered a No Code, No Resuscitation status. She barely responded to physical stimulation and not at all to voice, but showed signs of improvement. A chancy admission at best. However, her husband was very competent and devoted to taking her home no matter what. Even lessening the burden of care was a reach, but a possibility. Still, we knew we had a viable discharge plan with the husband, we proceeded on a matter of trust.

I had known the woman from earlier medical attendance to her over a number of years at my office. Numerous medical problems and not a lot of will to work, or spunk, she now was down to her last chance to gain a degree of independence. I was new to rehabilitation at the time, but I recognized a near 'basket case' if ever I saw one. She was one of the first patients admitted to our new unit, and now thousands of patients later, she stands out in memory.

In a frank discussion with her husband, I emphasized the hurdles that would have to be overcome, the constant caring, nursing, feeding, turning, toileting, respite, and other activities and services to be called upon over a very long period of time. Now that she had made something of a recovery and was no longer on 'No Code' status, she would live on. My mood and discussion verged well into the gloomy, guarded, and "we can only hope."

Her husband acknowledged that he would have a full time job in caring for Emily. They had no children or extended family to call upon. There were no tears, no hesitation, no qualifications, no exaggerated hope. Frankly, I thought both would be better off if she went to a nursing home. He would have none of it, a pledge I have heard many times since, but at the time I did not have the experience to know how seldom such dedication came to be manifest with our trust abandoned. He was not going to bail on us; that we could be sure of, trust maintained. Whether she was a suitable candidate for acute rehabilitation or not was problematic, spiced with a measure of naiveté, and finally, "Let's give it a try."

She arrived by guerney at 9:00 AM, our first day of operation. She was a two person, maximum assistance into bed, virtually helpless. By ten o'clock, Emily was in a dither, agitated, restless, incoherently demanding something, but we couldn't understand her well enough to discover what the matter might be. We adjusted the blankets, the pillows, the height of the bed, the lighting, the window shades, everything.

Still, she was not mollified. She was not angry, but something was amiss and we were missing what she had in mind. We had the nurses, one by one, and in the most caring and professional and personal manner, attend to Emily to try to discover what agitated her so. Nothing helped. Then, the nursing assistants. Nothing. The ward secretary. Nothing. Each of the therapists. Nothing. Her husband, if any one could understand what all the gesticulating was about, ever so patiently pried what he could from his wife. Nothing.

We were completely stumped. Our Recreation Therapist spent a long time with Emily, and after many tension filled minutes, brought forth the news: "Emily wants her hair done."

Emily was vain, not dead. Her husband said, "That sounds like Emily, I know her well, but I would not have guessed it."

Emily reached a tremulous hand up to her head, ran her bird-like fingers through her fragmented, reddish-brown hair, gone a little dull around the fringe.

It was an emergency. No expedient was spared. Every effort was brought to bear on Emily's hair. And, indeed, it was accomplished.

Emily made a wan smile. Her husband sat with her and held her hand, ignoring all obligations to self or others. The pink-haired hairdresser arrived. Emily sat up, tossed her shoulders a little, enough for her husband to notice. In a mellow state, she got the works: shampoo, set, cut, comb-out, a little color, prickly curlers wrapped in tissue paper, and her husband dispatched home to get her satin pillow case.

After that episode, everything was easy. After a few days, Emily was at breakfast in the dining room with other patients. A few more days and she stood on her own. By a week, she was took halting steps with the therapist, dressed herself, and before she went home, dazzled us all with her primping, and beaming side-long, went the full distance of the hallway on the arm of her proud husband. And soon, she was home. We knew we had a viable discharge plan. It was a matter of trust.

Surely, a therapeutic triumph. Our unit had no history, after all it was our first day, our first hour. She couldn't have heard about us, about our reputation because we had none. Accounting for Emily's recovery is not easy. I can produce no objective, scientific data for intense critical scrutiny or evidence-based medicine. Our therapies had not begun. Medicines played only a small role. When patients are admitted to a unit where expectations are high, they perform–most of the time. Maybe that was it. Or the 'Rehab Milieu' of trust.

Three years later, Emily experienced another illness that brought her back to our Rehabilitation Unit for another stay. Her husband was as attentive and reliable as ever. And Emily made it back home again. Neither Emily nor her husband would have it otherwise. Emily lived on for a number of years, and died in her sleep.

B. CATS AND DOGS: HOMESICKNESS

Ich will heim

Few situations occur that challenge trust more than a patient's homesickness. Most patients at some time during their stay in the hospital express a wish to return to home. In some instances, the pressure to return home becomes intense and not in the best interests of the patient at the time. When patients with brain injuries improve, just after the period of agitation but before a realistic awareness or return of reasonable cognitive abilities, a pathologic state of homesickness or excessive 'nostalgia' [from Greek *nostos* return *algos* pain] occurs. This period of nostalgia is associated with perseveration, a persistent demand to be released from the hospital.[1]

Homesickness involves separation from a familiar environment, and entrance into a new setting. Separation accompanied by perceived loss, interruption of plans, and withdrawal, leads to psychological disruption and compulsive

---

[1] Fred Davis. *Yearning for Yesterday: A Sociology of Nostalgia*. New York and London: Free Press, 1979; M.A.L. van Tilburg, A.J.J.M. Vingerhoets, and G.L. van Heck. "Homesickness: a review of the literature." *Psychological Medicine* 26 (1996) 899-912; Nicholas Dames. *Amnesic Selves: Nostalgia, Forgetting, and British Fiction, 1810-1870*. Oxford and New York: Oxford University Press, 2001; William Fiennes. *The Snow Geese: A Story of Home*. New York: Random House, 2002.

rumination about home. The new environment causes either strain and dissatisfaction in the individual or a commitment to participate. Information from the new environment competes with rumination about home. In 1688, German physician Johannes Hofer noted that homesickness could be a serious disorder, "many for whom means were lacking for a return to the native land, had gradually, with spirits exhausted, breathed out their life, and others had even fallen into delirium and finally mania itself."

In 1754, De Meyserey, a French military physician, recommended that homesick soldiers should be kept busy, their attention diverted, listen to music, occupied by tasks or participate in vigorous physical activity. In the most extreme cases, return to home rapidly cures homesickness, but not in the brain-injured patient.

So intense is the pleading of nostalgia that family members are easily caught-up in a patient's irrational wish to go home, such that trust in the medical staff is challenged by both patient and family. A family may be as insistent as the brain-injured patient on premature discharge from the hospital. Explanations on the nature of the medical problem may not suffice if the family is persuaded by the brain-injured patient to help him or her to leave the hospital. If the patient is discharged, or if the family takes the patient home against medical advice, the patient is an extremely hazardous behavior-risk since he or she usually has recovered ability to walk and other manual abilities when only days before they may have been in coma or severely agitated and still unreliable and unsafe.

In *pathological nostalgia*, an idealized and romanticized notion of the past overwhelms reason. Insistence on seeing their cats and dogs supercedes medical recommendations. Visits from pets may have a strange effect in that the homesick individual may reject or mistreat the longed-for pet during the visit.

Three stages of homesickness have been described: (a) exaggerated imagination of home as enchanting and delightful, (b) physical symptoms such as fever, GI upset, 'wandering pains,' (c) depression, listlessness, weeping and sometimes suicide. Distance lends enchantment with forgetting unpleasantness, and remembering only the desirable. Homesickness tends to be bitter-sweet, contagious and epidemic.

Several types of homesickness have been identified. The type most likely operative in the brain-injured patient is the 'primitive' homesickness found among primitive and mentally retarded persons who are excessively connected to their surroundings. Other types are an infantile or symbiotic homesickness occurs due to disruption of the primary connection with the mother figure in a mutually-dependent relationship; and a 'mentally-deficiency' homesickness due to a 'mental (or neurological) deficiency.'

Homesickness may be a serious impairment associated with many physical complaints, such as gastric disturbances, sleep disturbances, loss of appetite, headache, fatigue, and many other vague, ill-defined complaints. Obsessive thoughts about home and negative thoughts about the present environment occur with idealization of home. Withdrawal and apathy may occur with little interest in the new environment, but in the case of brain injury, patients restlessly pace and repeatedly question when can they go home, with little thought about what home is like.

Theoretical explanations for the distressing effects of homesickness include loss, interruption of life-style, reduced control, role change, self-consciousness, and conflict. Homesickness has been likened to a 'reversible bereavement.' Not knowing how to cope with demands of the new situation increases the perceived threat. Freedom of choice, or its absence, affects homesickness; those who leave home involuntarily are more likely to experience homesickness, likened to 'separation anxiety.' In military recruits, 'rigidity' best predicted occurrence of homesickness where individuals clung to old habits and life-style. In addition, neuroticism and lack of self-confidence increase the risk of homesickness. Homesick individuals seem to have a strong need for social support, but lack social skills to acquire it. Homesickness interacts with a host of other psychological states. Risk of homesickness increases if the individual perceives no trusted persons.

Intervention can be challenging to the Rehabilitation Team with little information or advice available for guidance. Homesickness in the brain-injured patient may be considered a primitive reflex or instinct and not a rational process. Thus, trying to convince the individual by common sense is futile. Gaining the patient's trust of one member of the rehabilitation team may be possible, so that the doctor, nurse, therapist, psychologist, or social worker is 'boss' which allows for a measure of organization. Allowing the individual to fantasize about conversations with those who are missed may alleviate pressures for a short time.

Distraction and activity often improve behavior. Physical activity that is repetitive and not necessarily useful but safe and easily monitored is best, but the activity must be extremely simple. Patients may participate in games, but usually when homesickness and perseveration on home is at its height, they are not cognitively able to engage. 'Thought-stopping' or time-outs gain a measure of relief to the staff, but re-direction must follow.

Control of the environment is essential in the agitated phase of brain injury: a quiet room without distractions from visitors, telephone, television, etc. with consistency of staffing as much as possible. At this stage, fear and near panic are the norm. As homesickness occurs, explaining repeatedly what has happened to the patient in the simplest terms over some days has a calming effect. Reassurance seems futile when the patient is coming out of the agitated phase of head injury, but patients gradually comprehend reassurance and become more trusting and redirectable.

Strangely, as the brain-injured patient improves by passing through the perservative into more organized phase of recovery, nostalgia or pathological homesickness tends to lessen. At this time, perseveration may be focused on things other than going home. Thus, it appears that pathological homesickness is a primitive instinct that is ordinarily controlled internally by the social instincts and maturation of the individual. In this sense, pathological homesickness resembles separation anxiety manifest in young children. Appeals to reason are ineffective, but distraction, physical activity, and gaining trust are beneficial.

C. 'CRISIS' AT 7 TO 10 DAYS: ITALIAN PROZAC

After a period of acute hospitalization, when testing, treatment and excitement of surgery and technical interventions are completed, patients may be admitted to the Rehabilitation Unit. The pace of activities changes, but not the intensity of therapies. At this point, the patient faces the day-to-day reality that whatever improvement may occur will take time: sometimes weeks to months. Each new day is much like the last. The difficulties of mobility or self-care change slowly during this period. Improvements in function come in small increments.

Family members grow impatient and want to help the patient do tasks that the patient is capable of doing himself or herself if given enough time to apply enough effort. Families see that rapid change is not to be and that they will be called upon to assist the patient once the patient is discharged to home.

A change comes over many patients at about seven to ten days. Some withdraw and refuse to participate in their therapies. Some refuse to eat or take their medicines. Others withdraw entirely, refusing to speak or give any sign of willingness to work at their own self-care. They may appear discouraged and depressed.

In some instances, patients become violent, throwing plates, food, medicines about the room. Cursing. Shouting. Swinging fists at those who would seek to help them, behavior aberrant to their usual nature, 'Hell-on-wheels' comes out in the little old ladies and frail old men. Family members may tell us that this is the way the patient reacted in the past to crises. Though seemingly calm and cooperative with the therapy staff, they say they have had enough. They are angry.

The medical staff of nurses and therapists becomes alarmed and calls for urgent and desperate measures to be taken to handle the crisis. The psychologist is called. The psychiatrist is called. Medicines to treat depression are often prescribed and doled out on schedule. Sometimes the patient becomes confused by the medicines and reacts in more negative ways. The crisis concerns everyone. Something terrible is amiss and must be addressed at once. One would think that no one should have a down-day, or a low period, or the blues.

The 'crisis' may actually signal or be a sign of improvement. That the individual has the awareness to become 'upset' is a call for rejoicing, in that he or she has the where-with-all to comprehend that the circumstances of their life have changed, and changed perhaps for all time. A reordering of assets and priorities must be accounted for in planning for the future.

"Italian Prozac" is what I call it, with deference to Italians or others who react openly and honestly. No cover-up. No beating around-the-bush. No nonsense. The individual has lost something of great value, some of who they are, some of their independence. Platitudes do not suffice. Psychotherapy does not help. Medicines often cause sedation and befuddlement worsening the situation. Sedation and tranquilizing medicines cause confusion and occasionally agitation that may bring more and more medicine. The family becomes distrustful, something dreadful has happened. The patriarch or matriarch of the family is throwing a fit, a torrent of anger and bombast, and everybody had better stand back or else.

Recognizing that the 'crisis' is a normal adaptive reaction to loss and working through it with patience and tolerance is called for, rather than unwarranted and ineffective consultations and drugs. Looking at the crisis without judgement and personal emotional involvement is counter to our natural manner. Demands to "Do something! Anything!" or other ill-advised interventions may take place.

Without medicine or other interventions except tolerance and understanding, the crisis passes in two to three days. Giving the patient the benefit and confidence of being able to handle some stresses without outside assistance gives them a sense of control and maintains their sense of pride.

In fact, if no reaction occurs at seven to ten days, or sometimes a little longer, may be an unfavorable sign, that the patient is too impaired to comprehend the gravity of their situation. Most people have coped successfully with distressing loses earlier in their life, such as adolescence when they gradually withdraw from the nurturing comforts of home to go out into the world. Or getting married or having children, with loss of the former status quo. Even the most sought after and welcome changes for the better mean the end of the comforts and security of the immediate past.

So we hail the crisis, we appreciate it, though it may be ever so trying for a time, the crisis is a welcome sign of progress. In fact, if the 'crisis' does not occur, it may signal greater cognitive impairment than otherwise thought present. Delaying or suppressing or blunting the reaction, the crisis, with medicines or trying to distract the patient's attention away from their troubles may prolong recovery.

Once the crisis is past, a new attitude develops. The patient becomes more cooperative, more willing to work and tolerate inconveniences and delays. Even under the circumstance of being in the hospital and in rehabilitation, a buoyant attitude often follows. They are now advocates for other patients and cheer them on. A new realistic attitude takes over that focuses on the future. With the gains that have occurred to bank on, the patient looks forward to making enough progress toward discharge goals, to leave the hospital more independent, knowing that more weeks and months of outpatient therapy may be ahead of them.

Time passes slowly when in the midst of a two to three week hospitalization on a Rehabilitation Unit. Every hour weighs heavily. Intrusive thoughts are inevitable. Worrying and fretting about an unknowable future, and the effect of loss of independence torment vacant hours. They have faced these situations before, and survived. They will do so again. In the meantime, the nights may be long. However, when patients return for a visit months later after discharge to home, they tell me that in retrospect their time on the Rehabilitation Unit seemed to pass in flash.

D. Family in Crisis

Much has been written about the family in crisis. A severe medical illness or injury is often only one of many trials that befall a family when a member of the family comes to the Rehabilitation Unit. Only then, when the social workers interview the family, does the extent of losses and travail come to the surface.

As stress becomes overwhelming, anger and distrust may be expressed. Resentment toward doctors, nurses, and therapy staff boils over. The tendency to reciprocate behavior cannot help, but maintaining an even temper and staying in control of one's self and allowing the patient or family member to talk is both therapeutic and preventive.

The outbursts of a family in crisis are not the same as a complaint. Rather, more a disburthening of intolerable troubles. Gently provoking or inviting the explosion of feeling is to be welcomed under these circumstances. Once the explosion has occurred and a little time passes, the outburst is usually followed by an apology and a measure of relief.

A truly distressed and "dysfunctional" family taxes all of our resources: doctors, nurses, psychologists, therapists, social workers, volunteers, and anyone else we can enlist to assist. At times, limiting our own losses is the best we can accomplish.

Troubles never come singly, "Good or bad, flowers or weeds, things seem to come in bunches."[2]

E. "SHE'S A FIGHTER"

"There's the respect / That makes calamity of so long life. / For who would bear the whips and scorns of time…"[3]

An elderly woman, "the old lady," hasn't much of a chance of gaining a great deal of independence. The middle-aged daughters standing firmly across the bed will not hear of it, and with a knowing smile say, "But Mom's a fighter!"

I look again at the patient, gray, wan, dried up, listless, sunken eyes, and wonder what she must have been like to leave such a memory in her children. A little more history comes out. She was always 'difficult,' that is, hard to get along with. Probably foreboding to a growing child.

Birdlike now, with shriveled fingers, talon-like fingernails. "She worked hard and made us work hard, too," say the daughters in a chorus. "That's right. Real hard." Nodding of heads in assent.

"Yep. She's fighter." They take a step or two back from the old lady's bedside, as if she were about to rise up and smack them across the knuckles.

Everyday, they come to the hospital to see the old lady. "There's still a lot of fight in her, Doc. Lot's of fight." Not the usual description of the family matriarch. Eight kids. They all come home for Thanksgiving. "Worked for days, getting the turkey just right. Plucked and everything. Oyster dressing. Made her own cranberry sauce. Her pumpkin pie won prizes at the State Fair."

The old lady groaned and shifted a little in bed. She hadn't said a word in days. "There. Did you see that? Trying to get up to the stove even now."

"She's got things to do, you know. Probably cussin the grocery man about the sweet potatoes not bein fresh."

---

[2] Boyajian. *Scholia Satyrica* 4 Winter (1978).
[3] *Hamlet* 3.1.69-71.

Nobody touches the old lady. Not without being wary, keeping an arm's length.

"You can trust her to do her part, Doc. She never gives up, you know."

She must be turned regularly to protect the skin on her backside. Wets herself.

"She's a fighter alright. She's a little weak cause she hasn't eaten much. She doesn't like the food. She was a good cook, I mean she's still a good cook. Baked her own bread. Kneaded the dough herself."

No reassurance was needed here. The old lady coughed and swallowed. The daughters jumped and looked on quickly.

Days passed. No sign of improvement. Still maximum assist. "She's a fighter. You'll see, give her a chance."

Hope upon hope, the old lady turned over in bed, faced to the wall, away from the imploring family. Worry came across the brows of the daughters.

"We must see progress for her to remain in acute rehabilitation."

"It's only a few days, now. She's a slow starter, but she's a fighter." The chorus again.

"It's time to make a decision about your mother. We've done what we can do. It's too much to ask her to work hard in the amount of therapy we must ask her to do."

Distrust in the staff or the doctors or the amount of therapy is voiced by the daughters. Defensiveness about the virtue of the old lady, like someone must bear the blame for failure of the stolid crabbiness in the old lady that carried her through her earlier chores.

"We'll never let her go to a nursing home. No way. Not an option. There's still fight in her. She'll wake up cussin any day now."

"Then perhaps she can be home with family care."

The daughters look at one another. "We can't let her go to a nursing home. She'd never forgive us."

"We would like for the family to come in and do all of her care to see if you can manage her at home."

The old lady's fight seemed not to be a family trait. They didn't show up.

So, the old lady's 'fight' was more abrasiveness, or irritability, or vociferousness, that might have looked like she was a fighter.

Strange to say, an old lady is described by the family in strong terms: "she's a fighter." But for old men, "he was on ornery, cantankerous, cussed old so-and-so." "Tough as an old boot." "Obstreperous!" is the rule.

No trust here. No sympathy. "Nope. He'll never give in. Always bull-headed." "Couldn't never reason with him once he got it in his mind."

As the family faces the fact that their assessment of the old lady or the old man does not measure up to their long-held feelings, they do not admit to themselves or to the therapy team that the 'fight' was primarily a grouchy and ill-tempered cussedness. These qualities do not translate into a maximum effort in time of illness.

Their disappointment may be expressed in accusations towards the rehabilitation team, or that the old lady wasn't given enough time or opportunity. Distrust takes over.

To be forewarned alerts the team to the situation, a situation that must be dealt with carefully. Every attempt to gain trust may be undermined by a passive expectation that the old lady will one day rise up swinging and yelling, like the old days.

About the old man, they say, "He was always difficult, so we don't expect cooperation or loving kindness out of him now." No revisionist affection for the old man, "...for they say an old man is twice a child."[4]

The end of the 'fighter' is a sad event. The memory of the stubborn or feisty parent is one of the casualties of time. Taking on the continuing care of the aged parent taxes the trust of everyone in the system.

F. THE VANISHING FAMILY

After a patient has completed his or her stay on the inpatient Rehabilitation Unit, the family takes over. One of the criteria for admission to Acute Rehabilitation is a reasonable discharge plan that requires involvement of the family or a responsible party to arrange for care post-discharge. When a family is given the discharge options available, such as admission to a nursing home, the family reacts with indignation, "Mother would *never* forgive us if we let her go to a nursing home." Family relationships and a heap of guilt enter into the decision.

As the rehabilitation process goes forward and progress toward discharge goals proceeds, but no miracle comes to pass, prior claims of devotion and dedication to the Old Lady or Old Man begin to fizzle. Often with a measure of distrust thrown in, veiled accusations about the reliability of care and alleged promises not kept, the family begins to pull away, and sometimes we lose contact with them; telephones not answered, messages not returned, appointments for family training missed, etc.

---

[4] *Hamlet* 2.2.380.

Although the family has been given advanced cautions about what can be accomplished with rehabilitation, they may confuse rehabilitation with resurrection or rejuvenation, and that they may mistake our goals with promises or guarantees. These warnings and cautions are set out prior to transfer to the Rehabilitation Unit, and reinforced soon after arrival, but may fail to be retained by the family who may be enjoying a welcome respite from caring for the little-old-lady who, rather than the vibrant and vigorous person claimed, had become a drain on the emotional and financial resources of the family.

Now, faced with the return of the aged patient, they see that they have not been granted amnesty, only a temporary reprieve.

As the time approached toward discharge back into the family's care, alarming and hidden maladies and disabilities begin to surface: bad back, bad heart, bad nerves come to the fore, bad temper, bad behavior, bad family dynamics. Bad relations.

Be on guard from the outset that the family may bail. Getting the family involved early and participating in care so they will see what care will be needed after discharge can gain trust and cooperation. In cases of doubt, a Family Day clarifies matters. In this case, the family does all of the care for the day under the supervision of the therapy staff, nursing, and medical management. Like any work of art, a point is reached when a decision must be made whether a project is worth going on with. So Rehabilitation. It depends on trust.

Everyone on the Rehabilitation Team must be involved with the family. Often, contact with family members occurs in the evenings and weekends when much of the regular staff is not on duty. Making special arrangements for meetings with the family at off-hours may help. No signal or warning signs flash at the beginning, putting extra pressure on those who make decisions of appropriateness for acute rehabilitation. Distrust by the family may spread to distrust of the admission coordinators by the therapy staff in the event of a problem discharge and a reluctant family. All must work together or the staff may become divided. No one can completely foretell who will and who won't progress as expected on the pre-admission evaluation. Nevertheless, the terms 'dumped' or 'sandbagged' arise if the patient proves not as able to participate in therapies and make projected progress towards discharge.

Maintaining trust in the event of less than optimal progress towards an acceptable level of independence is a challenge to all.

Chapter 8

PHYSICIANS AND CONFLICT

A. PHYSICIANS AND CONFLICT

Physicians don't like confrontations. Physicians have given away too much from the incursion of managed care and other impediments rather than engage in confrontations with the insurance industry. We receive no instruction in dealing with confrontations, complaints or distrust. Academic experience is of little assistance. Some academic physicians are claimed to have an 'early-warning system' in case of a complaint or if distrust should be in the neighborhood.

In Tolstoy's *Anna Karenina*, a scene occurs on a spring day during an outdoor lunch. A physician is accosted by a patient at his table during lunch. Why did the author use this scene? The doctor was perturbed, but lunch went on. Nevertheless, confrontations occur that physicians cannot avoid and must face.

No one technique or manner in handling confrontations works for everyone. Each physician must develop his or her own style given their individual attitudes and experiences.

One consultant physician in my acquaintance dealt with difficult or distrustful patients by provoking a skirmish, maneuvering the patient or family member into an argumentative state. In this way, since he was a master of debate or contention, he soon had them in the palm of his hand, under his control. It's a little risky, but for this physician, it worked like magic.

Another physician employed a mass of pithy aphorisms, sayings, slogans, expressions to calm the frothy waters of confrontation and in the process gain trust. He had an apothegm to match every situation, such as, "Not every tip leads to oil."

Other physicians bland the distrustful into submission. Some give in to every demand, which not possible under conditions of medicine where resources are to be spent for the greatest utility.

One physician used complex and incomprehensible or esoteric explanations full of empty rhetoric to soothe the furrowed brow of the dissatisfied and distrustful. These explanation would go on and on until the patient and relative wearied of the contest, and once they began to shift from foot to foot, they welcomed a cessation of verbiage, which soon came to a close.

At the worst, such encounters end with writing an unwarranted or unwise prescription, or at the very worst, performing an operation. Such desperation, justified by "I had to do something," though understandable, is unforgivable.

Attorneys understand confrontations better than physicians understand these human skirmishes since confrontations are a definition of much of what attorneys do. The cross-examination is confrontation institutionalized. In the absence of absolute truth, the strength or reliability of an idea, hypothesis or institution is only as great as its ability to withstand challenge, i.e. confrontation.

Being challenged and confronted by a distrustful patient or relative may be a disagreeable experience for most physicians. A challenge is also a chance and opportunity to establish the ground rules and gain the upper hand, to the benefit of both patient and physician, especially in gaining their trust. First, the physician must maintain control of himself or herself, knowing that confrontations are inevitable. In this war-of-words, logomachy, it is just that: words.

Words can be used to further the confrontation or words can be implemented to gain understanding and cooperation and trust. Words may be powerful, but they do not in themselves maim or kill. To sustain one's own argument and maintain an honest opinion, words must be used carefully.

We find on the Rehabilitation Unit we experience challenges and confrontations in numerous ways: from patients, families, insurance case managers, and other physicians. We take the challenge as an opportunity to make points for rehabilitation and sometimes to gain a sanction, and at the same time, we receive a great deal of favorable notice for our rehabilitation service. At one time, a challenge to the merit of certain therapies was brought against us. Rather than reacting defensively, we took it as a challenge to obtain a wider acceptance and understanding. Morale increased rather than being destroyed by proving ourselves against a serious challenge.

Taken correctly, a challenge or confrontation can be a blessing in disguise. A chance for validation of our services. A chance to gain trust.

Nevertheless, confrontations are not what we physicians savor. We would rather be free of such anxious encumbrances. Not every confrontation ends as a true confrontation, but once the concerns are out in the open, and dealt with like a complaint, the emotional aspect of the confrontation is defused. The confrontation becomes a 'meeting' in which both parties benefit. In the case when the physician becomes angry or disrespectful, the physician has lost, and regrettably so.

Treating the complaining, confrontational individual with respect and at the same time the physician maintaining control of himself or herself may work wonders, especially if the complainer has a reasonable basis for complaint. The evidence for the complaint that leads to confrontation may be ever so meager, but not to the patient or patient's family. If a misunderstanding leads to the confrontation, it cannot be resolved by anger or an arrogant attitude on the part of the physician or members of the rehabilitation team.

Confrontations are extreme forms of complaints. The method of dealing with complaints is applicable, even more so. In the case of repeated confrontations, the physician would be advised to have an intermediary present, an administrator or social worker. The confrontation is almost always worse to contemplate than to experience. Getting the matter taken care of as soon as possible saves a great deal of otherwise wasted time and energy.

B. FEAR

Distrust may be a masked manifestation of fear. Certainly, an emotional outburst with a defensive posture tends to ward off those about the patient or family. Especially in the case of confused or brain injured patients, as they become more aware, their behavior may escalate and become bizarre, restless, agitated or violent with fear underlying their behavior.

The expression of the eyes may be a clue with widely opened eyelids and sympathetic outpouring with cold palms, tachycardia, dilated pupils, and other manifestations of fear. When the patient has visitors, television, and telephone all going at the same time, the patient cannot process all of the sensory input, yet knows that something is going on that they cannot comprehend. The patient may appear at his or her most distrustful extreme during periods of fear that border on panic or terror. Uncontrollable restlessness or attempts at flight from the Rehabilitation Unit may occur if not promptly interpreted and managed.

By removing sensory stimulation as much as possible, patiently and quietly explaining why the patient may be afraid and fearful, the patient gradually comes to understand that their fear is due to something other than an actual physical threat. Reassurance must be repeated frequently until the patient has recovered sufficiently to be able to assess their environment reasonably themselves.

Families or friends who perceive the agitated behavior of the patient may aggravate an already difficult situation with panic in themselves. Thus, gaining the trust of family and visitors may be the biggest challenge. Explaining the nature of the patient's distress ordinarily quells the disturbance, but a distrustful family member or visitor may become agitated or abusive leading to escalation of the patient's behavior.

These situations tend to be highly emotional and disruptive to the Rehabilitation Unit, but usually quiet down with time. An histrionic visitor is usually a known quantity before admission of the patient to the Rehabilitation Unit and acquaintances give us a tip-off as to their prior behavior. To be forewarned requires the staff to act by being forearmed.

Although one's instinct is to reciprocate behavior with similar behavior, reciprocation of angry behavior must be resisted and a single experience teaches its counterproductive result. Remaining calm and in control under such circumstances draws on all resourcefulness and training of the staff. No two situations are exactly alike, but recognizing the setting and being prepared spares much distress and disturbance.

Adam Smith, in *An Inquiry into the Nature and Causes of The Wealth of Nations* (1776), says that the status of any profession is related to: "the amount of trust which must be exercised." Adam Smith points out the importance of the responsibility of the members of professions in the matter of trust:

> The wages of labour vary according to the small or great trust which must be reposed in the workmen. We trust our health to the physician; our fortune and sometimes our life and reputation to the lawyer and attorney.[1]

Adam Smith acknowledges the importance of trust and the necessarily one-sidedness of the physician-patient relationship expressed earlier.

John Ruskin (1819-1900), whose writings in the nineteenth century influence social theorists in the twentieth-first century notes the importance of trust in the physician:

> Not less is the respect we pay to the lawyer and physician, founded ultimately on their self-sacrifice...In the case of a physician, the ground of the honour we render him is clearer still. Whatever his science, we would shrink from him in horror if we found him regard his patient merely as subjects to experiment upon; much more, if we found that, receiving bribes

---

[1] Adam Smith. *An Inquiry into the Nature and Causes of The Wealth of Nations*. (1776) reprint. New York: The Modern Library, 1994,. pp 118-123.

from persons interested in their deaths, he was using his best skill to give poison in the mask of medicine.[2]

The support of medicine blends with the need for service, sacrifice, and trustworthiness in the face of criticism. Contemporary commentaries express similar sentiments. The issue of the cost of medical care is no longer absolute cost, rising costs or otherwise, but the return from such expenditure, i.e. value or trust in the work of the profession of medicine.[3] The physician who abrogates trust by complicity with cost reduction schemes to the detriment of patient care risks loss of public trust.

Society holds the medical doctor to a responsibility beyond that of a profession, beyond that of nearly all other professions. When vulnerable, the individual trusts, does not expect to be harmed, so that belief in another's good will goes unstated or understood. A trustworthy person cares, using discretionary powers wisely and responsibly, not to exploit vulnerability, neither excessively nor deficiently, while giving signs and assurances of trustworthiness.[4] The concept of trust in the physician-patient relationship involves individual physicians and the individual patient, not the institutions that surround them.[5]

Fear that the patient may not receive medical care that would be reasonable under present cost-control measures promotes fear in the public mind that trust in the profession is being compromised to the benefit of financial interests of businesses and governmental agencies. As one physician put it, to encourage a patient not to want medical services that financial agencies don't want to pay for. Money considerations have always hovered over medical care. It is unlikely that a change will occur anytime soon. In fact, cost pressures are expected to increase substantially as more people seek care of greater and greater complexity. In some instances, persecuting innocent physicians and medical institutions served to keep others in line by production of fear. Allaying fear and developing trust in an atmosphere that promotes fear and distrust will be a constant and important challenge to all members of society.

---

[2] John Ruskin. *Unto This Last*. (1862) Reprint. London: Penguin, 1985. p. 176.
[3] David Thompson, James Harrison, and James Flanagan. "From paradigms lost to paradigms regained? The MILTON approach to health care reform." *Journal of Management in Medicine* (1995) 21-34.
[4] Nancy Potter. "Discretionary Power, Lies, and Broken Trust: Justification and Discomfort." *Theoretical Medicine* 17 (1996) 329-352.
[5] Lee N. Newcomer. "Measures of Trust in Health Care." *Health Affairs* 16 (1997) 50-51.

C. "My Former Doctor"

Anthony Trollope, noted for his percipience on the vagaries of human nature, pitted Dr. Thorne and Dr. Fillgrave against each other in his novel *Doctor Thorne* (1858) illustrating the manipulative nature of distrust. The wealthy of Greshamsbury played the two doctors against each other, capriciously shifting from one to the other to watch the turmoil in the abandoned doctor. A patient received from one doctor was "taken as a victory" by the new doctor.

Occasionally, a new patient came to my office complaining about their former doctor who they disliked or claimed didn't take their complaints seriously, or in modern parlance "blew it off." Distrust flows from their criticism. Omniscience and absolute knowledge is what they expected, but, in the long run, the patient principally exhibited intolerance and distrust. The new doctor may be flattered and his ego inflated by these patients, that he or she will succeed where his colleagues failed. Yet, he knows that the former doctor is competent and occupies a high standing in the medical community.

A little experience taught me that when patients arrived at my office denouncing a former doctor, in all probability, I was next on their inventory of doctors to be abandoned, and they seldom became trusting or regular patients, but moved on to the next hapless medic.

Their words are ever so flattering and reassuring, that they are "good patients" and that I had been "highly recommended." Smiling, warm greetings, firm handshake. They know the ropes. Watch out! These folks tend not to be trusting, but manipulative, that with flattery they can con the doctor into compliance with their demands.

Not long after the above event, after having expended extra time and extraordinary effort in pleasing a 'good patient,' I received a request for transfer of records to a newer doctor. When starting my practice, these events were devastating to my sense of worth, ego, and professionalism. Later, I realized that these were difficult, distrustful, unappreciative people who left a trail of unpaid accounts, at my office and other offices and businesses.

Doctors tend not to discuss these deflating individuals with each other, but to suffer their demeaning behavior silently. On occasion, when comparing notes with close and trusted associates, I learn that they have the same experience and sometimes with the same individuals. No longer do I regret that my best efforts were not appreciated or accepted, but inwardly I am relieved that they have moved on. When I receive a letter requesting transfer of records, I no longer have a sense of failure or having "missed something," but feel relieved, the letter helps to enhance rather than diminish my office practice and myself.

On the other hand, when a new patient arrives and says, "I loved and trusted my former doctor, but I don't know about you." Initially, one tends to be taken aback, that such a blunt charge of doubt is hurled at me, but no more—it is a time for rejoicing! If the patient was able to trust and establish rapport with their doctor once, they are able to trust and establish rapport again. Uniformly, they become loyal and agreeable patients who will stay with their doctors through thick and thin, especially thick.

The distrustful can't be expected to change their stripes. Whatever they expect to accomplish by their base tactics I can't imagine. They are soon known throughout the neighborhood. These folks are on the police blotter as recidivists, "round up the usual suspects," and the shoplifter or pickpocket is apprehended. The distrustful, like the disagreeable cannot do otherwise, only attempt to be less so.

"Ill habits gather by unseen degrees, – / As brooks make rivers, rivers run to seas."[6]

D. "IF YOU WANT TO BE MY DOCTOR!"

Early in my days of medical practice, like other newly arrived physicians, a new doctor attracts patients from all directions. Most were reasonable and some difficult, but that is the territory whether a new doctor or a doctor established in practice. A few patients, who were initially agreeable people, when I raised questions about the need of certain tests or the appropriateness of medicines the patient requested, the patient in a greatly irritated state said, "If you want to be my doctor, you will order such and such!" No trust.

I was surprised and taken off-guard at such a response since I had known the patients for at least some time. At no time during my medical school or residency had anyone spoken to me in this manner.

Unprepared and inexperienced at these matters, I tried to appease someone who seemed to be a patient I didn't want to offend.

After a few similar experiences, these patients began to have a history with me. A history that was surprisingly constant. No matter how much I tried to please them, and do their bidding within reason, they drifted on to another

---

[6] Ovid. *Metamorphoses*. (ca A.D. 8) 15.155. tr. John Dryden.

doctor's practice. What they left behind them was a trail of bewilderment, frustration, and anger. Not the disappointment they must have counted on.

Now, years, decades, later, after having a number of equally frustrating experiences in dealing with the species, I am cautious of people, not suspicious, but ready to protect my own self-esteem if necessary.

I realized that this particular brand of humanity cannot be pleased without giving them title to all that I am supposed to protect, that a new approach was called for. The earlier the intervention the better.

I resolved that the next time a patient or family member said to me "If you want to be my doctor..." I will be prepared!

Since I know that they are already preparing their departure to another doctor's practice, I will grasp the advantage and I will say, very calmly, "Send me a signed authorization, and I will be pleased to forward your records to your new doctor." And end the conversation promptly. That is, hang up, since these encounters are entirely by telephone.

As I mentioned, these people were encountered in the very early days of practice, and clustered in a few years, and once I had determined what I would say the next it came up, strange to say, it has never happened again. Not once.

So again, people will treat us as we are willing to be treated. If we are to be their errand runners, then we will be sent on their errands. If we establish limits as to what we will accept and tolerate patients will regard us so, or move on. And, I say, to the consternation of some, the sooner the better.

What were the consequences? None whatsoever. The behavior described is three to four standard deviations off the norm. Statistically, I'd say, incurable. Cut losses. Save the day for better times and those who are amenable to human contact. No trust. No gratitude.

"Gratitude is a debt which usually goes on accumulating like blackmail; the more you pay, the more is exacted."[7]

E. FLATTERY

"He very good doctor! Look! Look! He very good doctor!"

Such remarks greeted me on entering a room spoken by the daughter of an elderly, severely disabled patient. The daughter scurried around, busily fussing about, moving the over-bed tray, the telephone, the bedcovers, etc. All a great

---

[7] Mark Twain. *Autobiography*. (1924), v. 1, ed A.B. Paine.

show. I had never before seen the patient or family. On and on the daughter gushed flattery and silly compliments.

I recognized the trap. And so it nearly turned out.

I replied, "We can only do what we can do. Much of recovery depends on the patient and the family. We cannot expect rejuvenation or reincarnation."

The flattery stopped. A glowering, hateful facial expression replaced trust like a sudden scene change in a Grade-B movie. Sullen and passively hostile, the daughter working her attempt to transfer responsibility onto the doctors and the hospital, and at the same time, set up a focal point for future shaming and blame-laying.

While some are prisoners of hope, this individual was out to search and destroy if the outcome of her aged and infirm mother was not to her illogical preconception and unrealistic expectations. Only magic could have changed the course of this patient's treatment, and her daughter, by magical thinking, expected more than could be reasonably expected.

Nothing is more destructive than a false hope. We can face most anything, even the worst, if we know what it is. Not knowing is worse. Reality seldom confronts us with travails worse than our fears or imaginations. How some of our patients survive what tragedies befall them is beyond my understanding. Somehow, they endure. Our responsibility is to be as accurate and forthright as possible under the circumstances. Most patients come around to trusting the therapy staff, and eventually trusting themselves and their families.

As the case of the woman above, the outcome was not favorable. No magic or reincarnation. The daughter behaved as expected, blaming and shaming the doctors and therapy staff. When reminded of limits expected, she sullenly relented somewhat. Had we fallen for her trap, she would have behaved vastly worse, degrading and threatening. I've witnessed that occurrence also. Reality was not to her liking. She was out to destroy, to maim, to draw blood revenge–revenge for an ancient injury.

While we try to gain as much independence as possible for each patient, some patients are over-mastered by their disease. The disappointed, as we have bitterly learned, behave as in past experiences. The therapy staff, nurses and doctors must carry on, to the next patient, the next storm. We cannot be destroyed by the hateful, entrapping and clever.

F. "And How Are *You*, Doctor?"

"And how are *you*, Doctor?" It's a nice sentiment, but be wary, a query that is followed by "we need you to be healthy." The patient is saying *sub rosa* that "you had better be here when I need you." And, perhaps, "Or else!"

More than a sincere interest in the welfare of the doctor, it is a public need that the doctor is viewed by the patient as being healthy, happy, unperturbed, and fully attentive.

I have discovered that the public will not tolerate two subjects of discussion: the doctor's personal health or ill-health, because it destroys public trust. No matter what, the doctor is best advised to keep his or her medical status out of patient communications. By all means, the doctor must not lay his or her burdens on those of patients, or tell patients' one's troubles. They have come to the doctor for their problems and care of their trouble, not the doctor's. Worse, patients tend to find the doctor's burdens unbelievable or boring. It is no way to enlist trust

Secondly, discussion of any money matters, medical financing, or personal finances with patients is usually a disaster. Mostly, they are unconcerned about the health and welfare of the doctor. The public has the perception that doctors are well off and above earthly cares, such as mortgages and loan payments. Such concerns are mortal cares, not a healer's burden. I began hearing it when I was a pre-medicine student. It goes like this: "So, you are going to be a doctor? Isn't that wonderful!" (pause) "And you are going to make a *lot* of money!" So often and repetitiously did I hear it, I began to believe it myself.

Even as graduate doctors, we hear the same sentiment. If we are not careful, we may fall into a trap of thinking that it is true, that whatever we earn is enough to make us rich. Only with experience and coming in contact with those in other lines of work, business or professions, do we find that we are more likely in a financial purgatory: we are not in hell, but we are not in financial heaven either.

For myself, I've made a living and a little bit more, but nothing that the well heeled would envy, even though they, too, have the notion of implied physician-wealth for the same reasons as everyone else.

To develop and maintain trust with the rich and the poor, I respond to the query "and, how are *you*, doctor?" by saying, "Just fine, thank you."

If they were to query, "do you have any worries or cares, doctor?" I reply, "Just fine, thank you."

Or if they inquire, "do you have any financial concerns, doctor?" I reply, "Just fine, thank you."

If they want to know if I have any trouble getting rid of all the money I make, I reply, "Just fine, thank you."

In order to maintain trust, the physician must appear unworried, healthy, and financially 'fit.' The public won't tolerate otherwise.

To inquiries suggesting the contrary, I reply, "I'm just fine, but, thanks anyway."

Chapter 9

CONCLUSIONS

A. THE SOCIALLY INEPT

Socially inept individuals have been with us for a very long time. We are not the first era to deal with those whom William Hazlitt (1778-1830), English journalist, critic, and essayist, refers to as 'disagreeable'[1]:

> Those people who are uncomfortable in themselves are disagreeable to others....This want of success is owing chiefly to something in what is called their *manner*; and this again has its foundation in a certain cross-grained and unsociable state of feeling on their part, which influences us, perhaps, without our distinctly adverting to it.

Hazlitt expands his observation of the socially inept:

> If we look about us, and ask who are the agreeable and disagreeable people in the world, we shall see that it does not so much depend on their virtues or vices–their understanding or stupidity–as on the degree of pleasure or pain they seem to feel in ordinary social intercourse....
> The more obnoxious the subject, the more are [the socially inept] charmed with it, converting their want of feeling into a proof of superiority to vulgar prejudice and squeamish affectation. But there is an unseemly exposure of the mind, as well as of the body. There are some objects that shock the sense, and cannot with propriety be mentioned: there are naked truths that offend the mind, and ought to be kept out of sight as much as possible. For human nature cannot bear to be too hardly pressed upon.

---

[1] William Hazlitt. *Selected Essays of William Hazlitt*. Editor Geoffrey Keynes. London: Nonesuch. New York: Random House, 1946. pp. 319-335.

The common denominator of these difficult, disagreeable, confrontational individuals is that they are 'socially inept.' They do not follow or obey common social conventions. The socially inept live in a primitive world recorded in Hobbes's *Leviathan*; *bellum omnium contra omnes*–the war of 'all against all,' leading to a life that is "solitary, poor, nasty, brutish, and short."[2]

When confronted by a trying, difficult individual whether patient, relative or visitor, one has little time to size up the situation and to set out in one's mind the principal characteristics that are encountered that must be dealt with. The 'final common pathway' is one of being 'socially inept.'

If in a movie or at the theater, these people would be played by George C. Scott, Jack Nicholson, Joan Rivers, Bette Midler, etc. Their behavior is three to four standard deviations off the norm. Their stories are told with the greatest of self-importance, *Sturm und Drang*, and hysteria reaching the level of absurdity.

Ordinary social graces don't work. Good morning. How are you? Did you sleep well? How was your breakfast? Similar social, agreeable opening salutations are met with a sullen silence, or a sour disagreeable response. The doctor, nurse, or therapist senses an attitude of disagreeableness and distrust in the patient. The awareness of the social ineptness of the patient is all that is necessary.

The next step is to decide whether the individual is socio-economically advantaged or socio-economically disadvantaged, which is usually not difficult. At the first encounter, most other considerations are secondary. The two groups of individuals are remarkably similar in their responses if they are one of the two or three per cent who consume ninety per cent of the energy in dealing with them. Even on the spur of the moment, this distinction is easily assessed.

In the case of the disadvantaged, keep it simple: no hello, no goodbye. Make your actions visible, concrete. Touch something, move something before addressing the patient or relative. Especially when you have advanced warning of erratic behavior, and especially on the first contact with the patient is this true. The same may hold true for the angry, difficult relatives or visitors. Many variations occur. One must be creative.

The socio-economically advantaged live by jargon and impressions, they are *over*-socialized. In this case, explanations must be laced with professional detail and *not* in simple terms. Understanding is not the initial goal, but gaining of trust. Again, this holds true only if they are among the two per cent who consume ninety per cent of the energy in dealing with them. A limit must be placed on the number of repetitive and senseless questions, but the use of terms they *don't* understand will give a measure of control, and gives the socio-economically

---

[2] Thomas Hobbes. *Leviathan–Parts One and Two*. (1651) Indianapolis: Bobbs-Merrill, 1958, p. 107.

advantaged a sense that they have been taken into *your* confidence. They will not ask you to explain what they clearly don't understand. If they do ask for an explanation, you have gained a position that they can trust. Then, and only then, can rapport be established so that actual education and information may be given to them. Later, with both socio-economically disadvantaged and advantaged individuals, genuine communication becomes possible. The therapy team must have control in this matter before the barriers of distrust can be breached.

The absurd, ludicrous behavior of the socio-economically advantaged and disadvantaged is followed by a grim nonsense. I tell my story with humor purposefully, not to insult or demean the socially inept, but a black-humor follows them once they leave the office or the hospital. Their wearisome 'outrageous' behavior no longer the threat or exasperation that it once was, the socially inept, like all other similar instances, must be dealt with by professional control and not reciprocal disagreeableness, which is not easy. Hazlitt, once again, says:

> What startles or shocks other people, is to them a sport–an amusing excitement–a filip to their constitutions; and from the bluntness of their perceptions, and a certain wilfulness of spirit, not being able to enter into the refined and agreeable, they make a merit of despising everything of the kind.

Nevertheless, Hazlitt was himself an extreme example of the 'socially inept' who was described by his father as "unfit for social intercourse," and by Samuel Taylor Coleridge as "singularly repulsive–brow-hanging, shoe-contemplative, strange"; he was jealous and quick to take offense, yet he had many friends and admirers.

The socially inept know who they are, and, strangely, are not offended when regarded as such. Though out of the norm of society, they may be interesting individuals, but do not change their manner, just as Hazlitt cautions:

> It is impossible for those who are naturally disagreeable ever to become otherwise. This is some consolation, as it might save the world of useless pains and anxiety. *"Desire to please, and you will infallibly please,"* is a true maxim; but it does not follow that it is in the power of all to practise it.... With this negative character he should be contented, and may build his fame and happiness on other things.

A sense of relief follows the socially inept, without much gained from the experience except stories to be related another day. Once they are gone, one has the feeling that since the episode is over, it won't happen again. In truth, it doesn't and it does. Each instance is unique, but certain common threads and yarns pass through all. Another patient or family with the same demands and outrageous behavior will arrive. It's part of the circus of medicine.

B. Ray Charles: "The Snake"

Jazz pianist and singer Ray Charles sings the ballad "The Snake" telling of a young woman, lonely, frustrated, estrus, and yearning. She finds a large snake in a deep snowdrift nearly frozen to death. She carefully takes the snake in her arms and carries it into her house, where she warms the snake by the hearth, feeds it broth, and lovingly cares for the pitiful, half-dead creature. Soothingly, she strokes the red and black and gold diamonds along the snake's head and back. She coos to the snake, rocks the snake, and sings to the snake. Happily and joyously she goes about her daily chores with a renewed spirit and physicality. She dedicates her days and energies to caring for the snake. She grows to love the snake. With greater and greater affection, she plays with the snake and the snake reciprocates in mutual trust and devotion by affectionately coiling its length about her arms and body and legs. The snake's health improves and slowly shows signs of recovery. The lonely young woman is delighted and heartened by its progress.

After some months, the snake completely recovers. The lonely young woman is thrilled, she is overjoyed. She dances easy rhythms with the snake, in a slow sort of ecstasy with the snake coiled about her, and tenderly sings of her dreams of wonderful days and thrilling nights ahead. They would travel and dine and dance and spend their days at exotic resorts and sailing to far off seas aboard luxurious ocean liners. They would live together in a wild uninhibited rapturous ecstasy.

Whereupon the snake savagely bites her between the breasts. Stunned, horrified, she drops the snake. She adored and loved and trusted the snake. Deeply wounded, she cries and wails in lament:

"How could you be so mean and treacherous, so deceitful and cruel?" she exclaims to the snake. "Had we not loved each other? Didn't we dream of our lives together forever?"

As the snake slithers and slinks away, it hisses back to the lonely young woman, "Be quiet woman, you knew I was a snake all along."

One can't expect a snake to change its ways.

My father, a veterinarian and wise to the ways of the world of both man and animal, said, "No use spanking the dog every time it messes on the rug. You can't blame a dog for being a dog."

William Hazlitt, again, reinforces that the tiger can't change its strips, "The utmost a disagreeable person can do is to hope, by care and study, to become less disagreeable than he is, and to pass unnoticed in society."[3]

No matter the effort in correcting, coaching, encouraging, some people are irremediable. Frustration and futility result from the patience and caring required to take care of these people. All manner of analysis is utterly useless and fails. Only their behavior can you hope to deal with and try to contain.

In the bigger scene, the functioning of the medical unit, office or center must go on. The socially inept threaten to undermine much of what the professions try to accomplish for our patients. Keeping one's sense of duty to the remainder of those in your trust remains important.

The snake was right. It knows who or what it is, and it behaves accordingly. You might say the snake was realistic. The lonely and longing, yearning young woman was a prisoner of hope. While life without hope may be intolerable, nothing is more destructive than to pursue a false hope.

While we strive for the best in all of our patients, some of our hopes will be undermined by those we most hope for. Hope and trust are not the same. Trust may be easier with hope, but hope does not require trust. Perhaps there is no such thing as a false trust. Maintaining a sense of the limits of what is possible while maintaining a sense of hope is a difficult, unsettling challenge. Yet, no other is at all satisfying. We cannot proceed without hope, within reasonable limits.

Though in most instances the behavior of the socially inept may be pathetic, to a great extent they are trapped by their own behavior, or their own disagreeable manner. What they most require is what they most reject. The distrustful come to the medical encounter distrusting; the circumstances of the moment do not change the truly socially inept. Though 'hope springs eternal' may be true; in the instance of the socially inept, eternally hope wilts.

"All men that are ruined, are ruined on the side of their natural propensities."[4]

C. A WORD FOR IT: REBARBATIVE

That disagreeable and socially inept people have been around for a long time is further demonstrated in the history of the vocabulary used to describe them. A

---

[3] William Hazlitt. *Selected Essays of William Hazlitt*. Editor Geoffrey Keynes. London: Nonesuch. New York: Random House, 1946. p. 334.
[4] Edmund Burke. *Letters on a Regicide Peace*. (1795-1797), p. 1.

few are given here from the *Oxford English Dictionary* including the date of first use:

threap: (ca. 897) King Ælfred. To rebuke, chide, scold, blame; to argue and bicker.

fulsome: (1375) Sc. *Leg. Saints. Julian*. Offensive to normal tastes or sensibilities; exciting aversion or repugnance, disgusting, repulsive, odious.

flagitious: (1382) Wyclif. *Macc*. Extremely wicked, criminal.

contumely: (1386) Chaucer. *Pars. T*. Insolent reproach or abuse, insulting or offensively contemptuous.

barratry: 1430. Lydg. *Chronicle of Troy*. Contentious, quarrelsome.

captious: (1447) Bohenham. *Seyntys*. Fallaceous, sophistical.

mordant: (1474) William Caxton. *Chesse II*. Caustic, biting, sarcastic, causing pain or smart, as wit or speaker.

BRABBLE: (c 1500) *Pore helpe*. To dispute captiously or obstinately, to cavil, quibble.

termagent: (1520) Dunbar. *Poems*. Overbearing, quarrelsome, blusterer, bully.

cavil: (1548) Udall. *Erasmus*. To object, dispute or find fault unfairly.

Mome: (English form of Greek Momus) (1563) *Mirr. Mag. Wilful Fall Blacksmith*. The god of censure and ridicule, fault-finder, carping critic, hypercritical.

choleric: (1583) Golding. *Calvin on Deut*. Inclined to wrath, irascible, hot-tempered, fiery.

tetchy: (1592) Shakespeare. *Rom. & Jul*. Quick to take offense, irritable, testy.

perfidious: (1598) Florio. *Perdido, Perfidiosa*. Guilty of breaking faith or confidence, basely treacherous, betrayal of trust.

contumaceous: (1603) Knolles. *Hist. Turks*. Contemning and obstinately resisting authority, stubbornly perverse, rebellious.

pervicacious: (1633) Ames. *Agst Cerem*. ii. Obstinate, stubborn, headstrong, willful, refractory.

atrabilious: (1651) Biggs. *New Dispensary*. Melancholy, splenetic, acrimonious.

invidious: (1661) Fuller. *Worthies*. To hold ill feelings or envy against another.

pawky: (1676) W. Row. *Contn. Blair's Autobiog*. Tricky, artful, cunning, crafty, shrewd.

fractious: (1725) De Foe. *Voyage Around the World*. Refractory, unruly; cross, fretful, peevish.

rebarbative: (14th Century). [Used in *Saturday Review* 1892 by Robert Coke]. Causing annoyance, irritation, or aversion, repellant.

gunching: (1949). [Not previously recorded]. Habitually complaining.

Willian Hazlitt put it together in modern prose:

> What signify all the good qualities any one possesses, if he is none the better for them himself? If the cause is so delightful, the effect ought to be so too. We enjoy a friend's society only in proportion as he is satisfied with ours. Even wit, however it may startle, is only agreeable as it is sheathed in good-humor.[5]

So, modern physicians and the medical and therapy staffs should not have to feel that if the tetchy and rebarbative individuals are tetchy and rebarbative that we have failed, and that their distress is entirely ours to balm, but that they are behaving in their normal, daily fashion and manner. And they know it. To change their basic behavior would be a monumental change in human nature, and no human endeavor is more human than the practice of medicine, even with all of our modern advances.

D. ADDITIONAL GUIDELINES

When presented with a socially inept or confrontational patient or relative, deal with behavior only. Don't try to analyze. It's no time to be understanding—you must take control.

Greet them with a firm handshake, a hard squeeze of the hand, not a limp, wimpy apology of a handshake. Use a strong voice in as deep a register you can muster. Speak a little loud, at least, no soft defensive talk. You are in charge.

Keep in mind that you are to relieve the distrustful and complaining of the responsibility of making a choice, to assist them in cooperating in making choices. Many people cannot tolerate the idea of freedom or liberty and react with distrust and resentment rather than a reasonable willingness to assist in decisions. Treat them like adults. Don't accept childish behavior. "When you can behave like an adult, we will talk again."

Above all, scrupulous honesty is an absolute requirement. The distrustful have their antennas out on red-alert for any hint of evasion or deception. Admitting and acknowledging error or oversight is best done as soon as possible, before the patient or family becomes aware of such an event. Oddly, admitting error heightens trust, not distrust, if carried out forthrightly and promptly. If the event is not handled appropriately, no amount of explanation will regain lost trust.

---

[5] William Hazlitt. *Selected Essays of William Hazlitt*. Editor Geoffrey Keynes. London: Nonesuch. New York: Random House, 1946. pp. 326-327.

With the disappearance of the middle socioeconomic class, more and more of the distrustful, confrontational, and socially inept will likely be with us in the future. As demand for medical services increases as expected and financial support for medical care does not, a bind is created that more must be provided with less. As the public becomes more aware, those who are socially inept and the Sybarites will likely be in greater numbers and more insistent on an already overtaxed professions of nursing, therapists, social workers, psychologists, administrators, and physicians.

A little humor may help, but the distrustful are not amenable to humor. Be careful. Humor can backfire. If you are not skilled at humor, don't try to use humor in these situations. By all means, be respectful and never allow remarks of any kind that might appear to be condescending or insulting and do not tolerate disrespectful remarks towards the staff or yourself.

Avoid labels, especially unflattering or judgmental labels for individuals who may be troublesome at the moment. Everyone has the potential to be difficult under certain circumstances. Better to assume that most people are reasonable most of the time. Only those who are way off the norm are to be handled in a particular way as detailed here. Although our goal is for patients to gain as much independence as possible, given their individual medical and social circumstances, paradoxically, we ask that they surrender some of the independence for a time in order to become more independent and safer at home in the long run: it is an investment in time.

A Few Additional Notes

Never stand directly in front of the confrontational individual, but to the side at a 45 degree angle. It is much more aggressive to confront an adversary when facing each other directly, but not from an angle. They may shift to stand directly in front again, but keep moving while making your change of posture appear to be a casual shift and not a retreat.

A table or bed or countertop may give them a strong embattlement from which to operate with utmost abandon and aggressiveness. Sitting across a table from them guarantees a prolonged, contentious, unfavorable outcome. The confrontationalist knows the battle plan that works best for them, so remove the safety barrier at the very beginning by sitting to the side of the table, or facing tangentially to the table. Sometimes, another person, friend or relative of the confrontationalist is seated between: an arrangement that must be altered. Excuse yourself from the room and upon returning, take a different seat or change its position. The intensity of rhetoric changes abruptly.

It's like a bullfight. On entering the bullring, the bull immediately establishes a safety zone where it is especially ferocious. The task of picador is to identify the safety area and to get the bull away from that spot where the bull is less confident.[6] So with management of difficult situations, maneuver the confrontationalist into a non-confrontational position as much as possible.

In management of distrustful, angry, and other individuals discussed, we must keep in mind safety of the patient and protection of the staff. Some people think that because we are in medicine that the medical and hospital staff are there to be abused and that they can take out their frustrations and anger on us, but we, too, have rights. Self-defense raises cries of paternalism from ethicists, that we should be able to endure any insult or aggressive behavior in doing our jobs. I disagree. If we are willing to be treated in a demeaning way, we will get more of it. When we say to ourselves, that's enough, we will take no more of such behavior, we are able to control it. If cooperation is not obtained in a brief and reasonable time, call for assistance.

Never speak about your own medical problems or discuss your own or your family's illnesses. In order to trust, the patient must feel that the therapist, nurse, doctor or others in the therapeutic setting are supernal, above earthly cares. Once you tell them of your mundane problems, you have lost a great advantage in gaining trust. Further, it is unprofessional and unfair to take a patient's time and trouble telling them of the doctor's or staff member's troubles to enlist their sympathies for those who are expressly positioned for the purpose of treating *their* ills. Few things destroy confidence and trust more quickly than a physician burdening a patient with a recital of their personal troubles.

E. CONCLUSION

No two situations are exactly alike; a certain amount of free-lancing, creativity and thinking on your feet is required. Nevertheless, enough general principles as noted here give one a method of dealing with distrustful and difficult people. At no time are patients, family or visitors to be treated in a demeaning or challenging way, but respectfully and firmly. Much more important that you tell *yourself* that you are not going to tolerate undermining and destructive behavior from patients and families. Some of the most difficult people if handled skillfully

---

[6] Ernest Hemingway. *Death in the Afternoon*. New York: Scribner, 1932.

may become your staunchest supporters and advocates. Everyone must develop his or her own style of coping with these troublesome, challenging situations.

Confronting the overbearing, bullying, threatening individual often is worse to contemplate than to experience. Once their intolerable behavior has been pointed out to them, they often give it up promptly, they realize their "cover has been blown" or that their actions don't work.

If all fails and the threatening individual is menacing, only one recourse is left: call for assistance, and sometimes call the guard. Calling the guard sometimes has an amazing calming effect. In my experience, it is never the first time that these individuals have exceeded limits, and the individual is almost relieved to be controlled. It's weird, but that's human nature in the raw. Whatever abusive behavior you are willing to take, you are going to get a lot more of it.

The distrustful and difficult individuals are fortunately a small per cent of patients. Not allowing their erratic behavior to disrupt the functioning of an office or a hospital unit or ward is essential. Especially important not to overlook are those agreeable and reasonable patients who work hard and never make a fuss about things that might not be perfect. They also deserve of our best efforts. We must make certain that their care is carried out to the fullest.

Trustworthiness cannot be taken for granted, but must be continually earned. Medical care never reaches the point of assuredness and the assumption of trust. By constantly being tested by the disagreeable, standards are shored up, not broken down or compromised. Our services and value to patients and community are validated in being challenged, even by the rebarbative and distrustful.

The ill will expressed by those in trying times and adversity must be taken in relation to their circumstances as well as their normal behavior. The advice of Gustave Le Bon, French physician and social observer, is ever appropriate:

> Memory of feelings exists as does that of intelligence, but to a much lesser degree. Time weakens it very quickly.... If memory of feelings were as tenacious as intellectual memory, the persistent remembrance of our sufferings would render life unendurable....An unnourished hatred does not endure....how quickly peoples who were former enemies forget hatreds not nourished....This concept of the essential brevity of affective memory explains many phenomena in the life of peoples. One must not count on their gratitude, but also one must not dread too much their hatred.[7]

---

[7] Gustave LeBon *Opinions and Beliefs (Les Opinions et les Croyances)* 1911. In Alice Widener. Le Bon: The Man and His Works. Indianapolis: Liberty Press, 1979, pp. 171-172.

Maintaining a sense of who we are and what we are called upon to do may seem obvious, but individual physicians, nurses, and therapists may have disparate opinions. Restating and including all medical staff in preparation of Core Values and Mission Statement of the individual units can be a unifying and reassuring process in maintaining standards of care in the face of challenge.

Prior to the twentieth century, diagnosis and treatment created a bond between doctor and patient. The development of scientific medicine in the late nineteenth century was greeted with a sense of awe. Scientific evidence eclipsed thoughts and feelings of the patients who grew increasingly ambivalent, shifting attention away from human concerns while increasing emotional distress. Cultivation of trust during times of great change is difficult. Society holds the medical doctor to a responsibility beyond that of a profession, beyond that of nearly all other professions—almost within the realm of supernatural belief; for the patient, a deep spiritual conviction about life and death which no correlative in medical science exists, such that patient and doctor often do not have a shared experience.[8]

The vulnerable individual trusts, does not expect to be harmed: belief in another's good will is understood. A trustworthy person cares, wisely using discretionary powers and acting responsibly, neither excessively nor deficiently, while giving assurances of trustworthiness.[9] Trust in the physician-patient relationship involves the individual physician and the individual patient, but not the institutions that surround them.[10]

Patient trust now is perceived as falling to an "alarming low" in both Britain and the United States. Most destructive to trust has been the "startling embrace" of the belief that competition in medicine produces maximal productivity. Nothing was more damaging to the 'trust' aspect of medicine than the belief that marketplace ethics and competition would improve medicine or make it less costly. In a profession where sensitivities of one's fellow man should be paramount, we are amazed and appalled, "absolutely bewildered," that so many physicians accepted a marketplace philosophy for the practice of medicine. Those who are basically trusting and permissive, and those who are distrustful and

---

[8] "The American Medical Doctor in the Current Milieu: A Matter of Trust." 2. *Perspectives in Biology and Medicine.* 37 (1994) 443-459.
[9] Nancy Potter. "Discretionary Power, Lies, and Broken Trust: Justification and Discomfort." *Theoretical Medicine* 17 (1996) 329-352.
[10] Lee N. Newcomer. "Measures of Trust in Health Care." *Health Affairs* 16 (1997) 50-51.

regulatory, have conflicting concepts of reality, and view each other suspiciously.[11]

New knowledge, increased education, and communication changed patients also. The spirit of the times is against authority.[12] Paternalism, or patient autonomy, is an exaggerated extreme that has no place in clinical medicine. Good medicine is and always has been based on mutual trust: trust that is earned, not given, and there are as many different ways of building trust as there are patients.[13]

---

[11] David E. Rogers. "On Trust: a basic building block for healing doctor-patient interactions." *Journal of the Royal Society of Medicine* 87 (1994) Suppl 22, 2-6.

[12] Joseph P. Horder "The historical perspective." *Journal of the Royal Society of Medicine* 87 (1994) Suppl 22, 9-9.

[13] Dame Margaret Turner-Warwick. "Paternalism versus patient autonomy." *Journal of the Royal Society of Medicine* 87 (1994) Suppl. 22, 16.

INDEX

A

absolutist, viii, 69, 70
abusive behavior, 114
acute rehabilitation unit, 1, 2
acute rehabilitation, 1, 2, 30, 91, 92
alternative medicine, 11, 66-68
ambivalence, 77
anger, 5, 20, 24, 25, 27-30, 32, 36, 43, 49, 50, 54, 55, 58, 59, 64, 65, 70, 74, 79, 87, 88, 95, 100, 113
angry behavior, 25, 96
anxieties, 12, 80
anxiety, 20, 48, 70, 78, 80, 85, 86, 107
argumentum ignoratiam, 69

B

backward causation, 77
behavioral problems, 1
Big Shot from Out of Town (BSFOT), xiii, 51-53
bi-modal society, 5
borderline individual, 78, 79, 80
borderline patients, 80
borderline personality, 78
bounded rationality, viii, 71, 72
brain-injured patient, 84, 85, 86
bullying, 31, 37, 38, 114

C

chaotic behavior, 2
Charles, Ray, viii, 108
check-ups, 61
children, 4, 14, 78, 81, 86, 87, 89
communication, 1, 13, 16, 32, 33, 36, 107, 116
competitiveness, 11
complainers, 19
complaints, 9, 11, 18-22, 24, 26, 28, 29, 33, 50, 62, 67, 85, 93, 95, 98
confidence, 8, 11, 12, 23, 24, 27, 42, 45, 50, 59, 61-64, 85, 87, 107, 110, 113
conflicting concepts, 116
confrontationalists/confrontationists, 38, 52
confrontations, 28, 39, 93-95
contamination, 77
control of anger, 79
core values and mission statement, 115
crisis, 7, 25, 79, 87, 88
criticism, 24, 30, 36, 54, 97, 98
cultural values, 78

D

depression, 79, 80, 84, 87
destroying trust, 44, 73

destructive behavior, 73, 113
development of trust, 1
Dickens, Charles, 31, 38, 46
difficult patients, 39
difficult people, xiii, 2, 23, 113
disadvantaged patients, 13, 14
disgust, 24, 76, 77, 78
distressing effects of homesickness, 85
distrust, xiii, 2-4, 7, 8, 10, 12, 13, 16, 18, 20, 32, 33, 35, 44, 45, 47, 48, 50, 54, 64-68, 73, 76-78, 88, 91-93, 97, 98, 106, 107, 111
distrustful people, 4, 43
distrustfulness, 20
Dooney-Bourke Boundry, viii, 75, 76

E

educational information, 4
entitled demanders, 40
envy, 58, 73, 102, 110
ethics, 3, 80, 115
extended family, 3, 81

F

families, xiii, 1, 2, 5, 13, 14, 16, 29, 32, 42, 52, 54, 66, 68, 69, 76, 94, 101, 113
family conference, 75
family in crisis, 88
family members, xiii, 2, 18, 30, 56, 59, 67, 78, 84, 92
famous person, viii, 53
fears, 12, 57, 101
flattery, 98, 101
frustration, 2, 25, 27, 29, 32, 33, 35, 36, 50, 54, 59, 100

G

gratitude, xi, 9, 12, 15, 17, 28, 39, 41, 51, 55, 64, 76, 80, 100, 114
guilt, 8, 10, 40, 49, 50, 57-59, 91

H

habitual complaining, 29
hate, 30, 50, 59, 73, 74
hateful patients, 39, 40
Hazlitt, William, 38, 105, 109, 111
Help-Rejecting Complainer (HRC), 26
Help-Rejecting Complainer (HRC), 26, 27, 28
hierarchical social systems, 4
hierarchical social welfare system, 13
HMOs, 11
homesickness, 83-86
hospitalization, 20, 66, 86, 88
hospitalized patients, 15
hostility, 20, 33, 36, 40, 70, 74
human behavior, 2, 8
human interaction, 2, 36
human nature, 2, 18, 36, 74, 98, 105, 111, 114

I

impulsiveness, 78, 79
insurance, 9, 11, 29, 51, 52, 61, 65, 71, 93, 94
Intensive Care Unit (ICU), 3, 4
interpersonal relationships, 78
interventions, 3, 86, 87
intimidation, 31, 37, 38, 40, 46
intimidators, 37-39, 52, 65
Italian Prozac, viii, 86, 87

J

jealousy, 73

L

language, 12, 13, 15, 16, 22-25, 30, 31, 36, 46
legal tablet, 18

M

Machiavelli phenomenon, 55
magical entitlement, 40
managed care monster, vii, 44, 45
managed care, 11, 44, 45, 63, 64, 93
mania, 84
mass behavior, 73
Medicaid, vii, 11-13
medical care, 29, 40, 44, 45, 52, 66, 74, 78, 97, 112
medical expenses, 11
medical providers, 1, 67
medical services, xiv, 5, 97, 112
medical staff, 1, 8, 12, 22, 25, 39, 43, 50, 51, 53, 66, 84, 87, 115
Medicare, 11
menacing, 30, 114
mental health, 80
middle class, 5, 14, 50
middle incomes, 5
modus vivendi, 10, 33, 35, 49, 66
mood changes, 79
mood disorders, 78

N

neglected parent constellation, 49, 51
nursing home, 82, 90, 91

O

out-of-town Sybarite, 49, 51
outpatient therapy, 88
outrageous behavior, 39, 108

P

pain society, 67
passive helper, 29
paternalism, 4, 113, 116
pathological nostalgia, 84
patient care, 41, 52, 97
patient management, xiv
personal contamination, 77

personality conflict, 74
physician-patient relationship, 7, 10, 16, 62, 96, 97, 115
popular opinion, 69
postmodernism, 67
pride, 16, 22, 60, 68, 87
problematic situations, xiv
psychological distress, 79
Public Relations Department, 52

Q

Quality Assurance Office, 9, 49

R

rage, 12
reasonable behavior, 29, 32, 73
reasoning, 1, 72
reciprocal altruism, xiv
recording devices, 16
recovery, 10, 50, 51, 52, 69, 81, 83, 86, 88, 101, 108
recreation therapist, 82
rehab milieu, viii, 81, 83
rehabilitation team, xi, 85, 92
rehabilitation unit (rehab unit), xiii, 4, 8, 29, 30, 50, 52, 64, 65, 74, 75, 81, 83, 86, 88, 91, 92, 94-96
rehabilitation, 30, 59, 66, 68, 81, 82, 85, 88, 90-92, 94, 95

S

schmoos, 43
scientific claims, 2
self-care, 86
self-esteem, 27, 100
self-image, 79
self-importance, 106
sensory stimulation, 95
shame, 50, 57, 58, 59
shaming, 58, 59, 101
sick-sybarite syndrome, vii, xiii, 6
sick-Sybarite, 9, 10, 11, 31, 32

social conversation, 18, 42
social ineptness, 106
social roles, 57
social worker(s), 85, 88, 89, 95, 112
socially inept individuals, 105
socially inept, 40, 52, 55, 65, 105-107, 109, 111, 112
socio-economically advantaged, 4, 6, 106, 107
socio-economically disadvantaged, 4, 11, 13-15, 106, 107
splitters, viii, 64-66
squatter(s), viii, 64-66
staff morale, xiii, 65
standard deviations, 2, 39, 55, 100, 106
student health center, 63
Sybarite, vii, viii, xiii, 6-12, 31-33, 49-51, 78, 112
sympathetic magic, 77

T

telephone terrorist, vii, 45, 46
temper, 79, 88, 92
therapeutic efforts, 20
therapeutic plans, 27, 29
therapeutic relationship, xiii
therapeutic setting, 19, 113
therapeutic situation, 20, 28, 31, 47, 59
therapy staff, 5, 8, 20, 22, 23, 39, 45-47, 52, 59, 64, 65, 73, 75, 76, 86, 88, 92, 101
therapy team, 19, 20, 23, 39-41, 45, 60, 75, 79, 80, 91, 107
thought-stopping, 85

threatening behavior, 31
threatening individuals, 2
time-victim card, 33
toxic healthcare professional, viii, xiii, 54, 55
toxic intern syndrome, 54
transfer of records, 74
trauma service, 13
types of homesickness, 84

U

unwelcome visitors, 42
utilization committee, 66

V

victimization, 42
violence, 25, 26, 43, 58
virulent visitors, xiii, 41
vocabulary, 109
Vuitton, Louis, 6

W

welfare of the doctor, 102
welfare system, 13, 14
well-meaning visitors, 42
why-negation complex, 32, 33
why-question, 59

Y

yellow tablet(s), 11, 15-18, 55